Disclaimer:

This book relates the events surrounding the author's experiment in self-medication with lysergic acid diethylamide, or, as it is more commonly known, LSD. It is a criminal offense in the United States and many other countries, punishable by imprisonment and / or fines; to manufacture, possess, or supply LSD. You should therefore understand that this book is intended for entertainment and the sharing of information and not intended to encourage you to break the law. Notwithstanding the legality or illegality of the treatment in question, no attempt at self-diagnosis or self-treatment for serious or long-term mental or physical problems should be made without first consulting a qualified medical practitioner. The author and the publisher expressly disclaim any liability, loss, or risk, personal or otherwise, that is incurred as a consequence, directly or indirectly, of the use and application of any contents of this book.

DEDICATION

The writing and publishing of this book would not have been possible without the enduring support of my parents, who've supported me throughout my entire journey; through so many moments of hopelessness, confusion, and despair; so many drawn up and redrawn up plans for helping me live independently; so many visits to this doctor or that doctor for this medication or that medication. Through all of this, they've been there. And today, I'm grateful to be able to be here, to say to them, to the world, that I've survived. I've survived the hand I've been dealt. I've joined the lucky few who get the chance to discover and understand their place in the hedge maze of mental illness. I've survived thoughts of brokenness, and adopted feelings of acceptance. And while yes, LSD played a significant role in my journey toward growth and acceptance, it was my parents who were there for me in the ways I needed most. They helped to create a safe space in which I could talk about and explore my condition, and overcome so many of the formerly obscured and fully unseen obstacles in my life.

So thank you, Mom and Dad. Thank you. You've supported me this whole time, including the times in which I mentioned experimenting with very, very illegal things. Thank you. Thank you. Thank you.

I love you,
-Aaron

INTRODUCTION

Hi. My name is Aaron.

At the age of 23 I was diagnosed with Autism Spectrum Disorder (ASD). At the age of 27, I was given Lysergic Acid Diethylamide (LSD). And to make a very long story short: when LSD met my ASD, I experienced incomparable relief for — and, in some sense, a near-total resolution of — my struggles with Autism Spectrum Disorder. The previous statement is significant, and worthy of a great deal of clarification. So let me first start off by saying that a dose of LSD does not "cure" my condition, in the way one takes an antibiotic and gets well. Even so, on LSD, my otherwise confusing and overwhelming ASD-related sensory issues seem suddenly manageable. My mind stills. My awareness widens. And my typically obscured ASD-affected outlook shifts from seeming vague and muted to instead feeling readily accessible, orderly, and deeply sensed in a way that allows me to navigate my life, and feel my way forward in a way that was previously impossible before I met LSD.

On LSD, I can read between the lines of social interaction, in ways I quite literally could have never imagined. I can detect and forge new associations between novel, newly accessible external stimuli and novel, newly accessible internal sensations. In this way, LSD transforms me from an autistic individual blind to select subsets of stimuli into an autistic individual who can not only see more, but also — critically — feel and process more, period.

I have spent hundreds of days living life with LSD molecules bound to my 5-HT2A receptors. And based on my experiences in terms of both microdosing as well as dosing in larger quantities, I would say without hesitation that LSD serves as a "neurological contact lens" that helps me, an ASD-affected individual, see the world more clearly. In specific, LSD allows me to perceive and feel and process and navigate sensory information critical to social and emotional navigation in a way that would have been previously impossible for me to perceive and process in my pre-LSD life.

And I know. I know. It sounds too good to be true. And anyone who hasn't experienced this particular shift in perception could and should be skeptical. I'm still trying to wrap my head around it, too. But that's why I've written this book. This is an attempt to describe my experience. Yes. But this isn't a declaration so much as it is the start of a conversation. My deep-dive into the academic literature and published research leaves me with a sense that while there are some potential explanations for this foundational shift in my subjective experience, there is still a lot to explore and research from a neuropharmacological perspective. And that's why I've written this text, in hopes that my first-hand account can inform a more rigorous, evidence-based body of research.

Another critical reminder before we begin: I am not a doctor, nor am I a neuroscientist. And for those of you out there who hold expertise in the relative domains of psychology, neuroscience, pharmacology, occupational or behavioral therapy, etc., I humbly say to you, "Hey, can you help us figure this out?"... And for those of you who do not hold any specialized degree apart from a masters in your own life experience, I ask, "Hey, have you or anyone else you know ever experienced anything like this?" Because I need help with this exploration of both ASD and LSD. A sample size of 1 is far from scientifically rigorous. And I know that. But even so, my particular experiences and self-healings seem far too remarkable and important to leave unshared. And so we come to the short, short version of my ever-evolving hypothesis. Here's the abstract I've got so far...

– – –

In basic terms, ASD has been theorized to be the result of disconnected or weakly-formed connections — and, in turn — weak cross-communication between key processing networks of the brain. In similarly basic terms, LSD has been shown to synesthetically connect otherwise disconnected or weakly connected processing networks of the brain, including networks theorized to play a key role in autism. With this in mind, my underlying thesis — as strongly supported by my direct experiences on and off of LSD, and increasingly supported by the new wave of published fMRI-imaging studies of both LSD and ASD — revolves around the notion that LSD can be the neurological amplifier and connective patch that enables ASD-affected individuals to perceive and navigate the world through a more harmonious, neurotypical-like processing lens.

Once again, I am not a doctor. Yes, I have read hundreds of scholarly works detailing my disorder in addition to reading every possible word I can find related to the neural signatures and the potential mechanisms of action of both ASD and LSD. But again, I am not a doctor. I am not a certified neuropsychopharmacologist.

I've read all of these academic works with such an obsessive fervor for two reasons: (1) my ASD predisposes me to having a penchant for repeatedly focusing on highly specific special interests, and (2), as a result of my neurochemical epiphany, I've deemed it critical to fully and forever dedicate myself to the task of reaching an understanding of how it came to be that LSD enabled my autistic mind to perceive and process that which my autistic mind was previously blind to perceiving and processing.

The first step in the journey toward scientific comprehension and eventual evidence-based validation is to share my story, and to likewise describe, from a subjective standpoint, what it means to be me, an individual affected by ASD, both with and without LSD in my system. Because maybe just maybe if I can manage to describe these shifts in perception, then maybe just maybe I can inspire others to collaborate in pursuit of new and better questions and new, better answers — answers that can then be leveraged for developing therapeutic and medicinal applications for LSD.

So, here's how this book will go.

First, I'll describe what life was like for me as an ASD-affected individual before encountering LSD. Then I'll describe the details of my first sensory-awakening experience with LSD, followed by the process of integrating some of the most influential insights into my day-to-day life. After some additional reflections upon my identity as an autistic individual,

I'll then spend some time unpacking my self-refined methodologies, including explorations of my practice of microdosing with LSD as a means of SSRI replacement, as well as my self-guided exploration of empathic attunement through an approach I refer to as LSD-Assisted Immersion Therapy. Finally, we'll wrap up with a quick headline-level look at the neuropsychopharmacological intersection of ASD and LSD research, capped off with a few quotes from the pre-prohibition era of research, as well as the so-called "psychedelic renaissance" unfolding in these modern times.

One last thing before we begin. I've been researching and writing about this stumbled-upon phenomenon for the better part of 5 years, hesitating with publishing out of a fear of judgement and general misunderstanding. But that was then and this is now. And the public perception of paradigm-shifting medicines such as LSD and psilocybin seems to have come a long way in a very short time thanks to a massive influx of donor capital and an uptick in evidence-based advocacy and exploration to match.

For evidence of this shift away from stigma and toward scientific understanding, consider this: on the very morning I typed this sentence you're reading right now, John Hopkins announced the opening of a modern psychedelic research center, joining countless organizations around the world in the revisiting of research that began some years ago, prior to prohibition.

After decades of first-hand accounts told and underground success stories lived, many more are speaking publicly in regards to their remarkable transformations. And so it goes that I release my words to the world, believing that the potential public benefit — to the domains of neuroscience, neuropharmacology, autism research, and mental health research at large — assuredly outweighs any potential detriment to my personal reputation and future.

I stand by my words. I do not fear ridicule. And I am so grateful that you're reading this. Because it means we are both one step closer to understanding one another in ways we might never have been able to otherwise imagine.

Oh and one last thing:

When Ben Franklin's kite got hit by lightning, he didn't go around saying "Hey everyone! Go fly a kite in a lightning storm!" No. He said "Interesting, maybe there's some scientific principles at play. Let's explore that." And that's what I'm saying. Something unexpected happened to me. And so, let's explore. Let's explore the possible mechanisms of action. Let's explore the possible medicinal and therapeutic applications. Let's explore. Let's explore. Let's explore.

Thanks for reading this.
Thanks for your Emails.
Thank you.

-Aaron

CHAPTER ONE

M E   B E F O R E   L S D

To be me...to see through the eyes of my autistic mind (before I met LSD), meant experiencing the world in the form of fragmented bits of vague sensory data; muted and obscured cues that ultimately still required a great deal of manual assembly, by me, the observer, over and over, on the Lego-block play table of my mind. It felt like I was Lucille Ball in that chocolate factory sketch, and whatever chocolates my mind couldn't seem to box seemed to wholly escape my awareness, which seemed to make my waking view of the world rather incomplete, blurred around the edges, blind to what may dwell outside of my narrow frame of perception. And while this experiential summary may sound like an explanation of anyone's waking awareness — autistic or not — I believe that my autistic awareness predisposed me to being especially blind to very particular aspects of experience; specifically, sensory data crucial to social and emotional intuition, and in turn, the navigation of the social and emotional landscapes of my life.

In this way, the majority of my pre-LSD-life seemed to be limited by a self-evident absence of emotional awareness and empathetic access. Processing deficiencies such as these have been shown to be common among individuals on the autism spectrum. But even so, I remind us that these exact traits don't necessarily define ASD in and of themselves, because as we know, autism is a spectrum, and no two autistic brains are exactly alike.

Before I had taken any LSD in my life, my apparently particular deafened and dulled ability to read and perceive the intention and tone and emotional state of those around me left me feeling confused, often. In most cases, this social blindness could be masked or covered up by my reliance upon learned routines or memorized scripts. But all too often, my maps and routines failed to serve me, outing me as a tone-deaf socializer, well-versed in the recommended chord progressions but woefully incapable of hearing the backing rhythm, much less harmonizing with other instrumentalists in the jam sessions of social interaction.

In some sense, I used to always feel like a forensic socializer; as though I had to make intellectual sense of my social experiences for the simple reason that my emotional intuition seemed to be absent in a general sense prior to LSD. And that meant that the processing speed of my social interpretations of the world usually lagged in comparison to the processing speed necessary for seamless social exchanges.

To give you an example of what I mean, consider this: before LSD, if someone had approached me and said "I'm so happy it is raining outside", my mental construction yard often became immediately and aggressively overwhelmed by an abundance of poorly woven-together bits of sensory information. I would have to process the symbolic literal meaning of the phrase "I'm so happy it is raining outside". I would then have to cross reference that phrase with the current circumstances within which I found myself. At the same time, I would have to process the inflection, and then cross-reference said inflection with memories of times I'd heard the sentence uttered in the past. If I hadn't heard the sentence in the past, I would then have to cross-reference the intonation, which, when combined with visual information derived from facial movements and posture, combined to provide some clue into the essence of what said person was saying to me. As evidenced by this very long paragraph that you're currently reading now, all of this laborious manual processing and recall almost always seemed to move slower than the speed of social exchange. In other words: while I was busy devoting mental energy and time to arriving at an apt interpretation, I was likewise forced to abandon my post in terms of how I myself was wearing/puppeteering my face/body/voice, etc. And so, even something as small as someone coming up to me and saying "I'm so happy it is raining outside" quickly became a mental quagmire.

All of this impaired social navigation seemed a bit like trying to play improvised jazz from memory rather than intuition. Sure, it "worked", but the moment someone went off-script, my expressive disharmony made itself known almost immediately.

I am in no way joking when I say that before LSD, I felt more closely related to a robot or robotic learning algorithm than I did to a human being. In some sense, I had always felt forced to behave and grow like an A.I., as though I was a self-learning Roomba Vacuum Cleaner, bumping into conversational faux-pas as if they were couch legs; slowly learning the map of the living room of human beings but never truly feeling or perceiving the true nature of the living room of human beings.

The aforementioned issues with processing the signals in the noise seemed to be most pronounced in situations in which I was dealing with in-person conversation, most especially when I was attempting to interpret the abundance of sensory information found at large social gatherings. But I want to be clear about this and say that even without LSD, I seemed to have SOME means of figuring out what was happening. I could discern what seemed to be happening, to a degree, but the social and emotional processing felt exhausting, less accurate, and less successful in terms of yielding mutually beneficial results for all persons involved in a given exchange.

I realize I'm being a bit repetitive here but I'm doing so for the sake of more completely articulating an otherwise abstract and wholly subjective experience. So to say this another way: before LSD, any sense of connectedness relative to my human experience seemed to only occur on the other side of deductive reasoning, in the abstract reconstructions and images of my mind, rather than the felt space of the body. And this experience seems to be rooted in my autism-specific dominance of cognitive empathetic processing, paired with an impaired theory of mind, versus the emotional empathetic processing more common in neurotypical individuals who can typically more readily demonstrate theory of mind.

Before LSD, I clumsily navigated the world, constantly assembling otherwise disassembled clues, trying to make a mental note of the paths that yielded penalties or rewards, all in an effort to arrive at "proper action", not realizing that the answers to social situations were hidden just beyond the reach of my obscured autistic perception. This type of memorization-dependent, do-this-then-that style of learning was useful for achieving on-paper successes, in school, or in front of a computer. Sure. But at the same time, this form of do-this-then-that learning was not so great for participating in a redeeming social existence. Because any new or novel experience that deviated from memorized flowcharts left me grasping for explanations. And once again I emphasize that before LSD, I was fully unaware that the clues and answers were hidden in plain sight, on the faces of those around me, in the tones of their voice, the positioning of their bodies. Because indeed before LSD I was mainly interpreting my experiences through the memorized maps of the past, rather than the sensory information of the present.

In saying that I seemed to be especially socially unaware, it is not to say that I was completely blind before LSD. It's more so that, before LSD, I had exactly zero experience with living a life in which kinesthetic empathetic feelings could be experienced so directly. And because of this, connecting all of the dots was likewise tremendously difficult if not impossible, because although I could see a smile, I didn't sense nor know, intimately, the warm, felt sensation engendered by the sight of that smile.

Before LSD, it seemed to be that if I was watching a movie, I would only be able to interpret the expressions of the actors from a deductive perspective. Like... I wouldn't viscerally feel the emotional states of the actors on screen, but I could guess about the emotional states using words that describe the visual clues. I could deduce that the actor's smile

= the actor is happy. I could deduce that the actor's laughter = joy. But I wouldn't intuitively feel nor sense the actor's emotional state in my pre-LSD years.

Likewise, before LSD, as both a child and young adult, I would see humans and talk at humans and listen to humans. I would LEARN ABOUT the humans. I would LEARN ABOUT the things the humans did. I would LEARN ABOUT where the humans were born. I would LEARN ABOUT what the humans liked or didn't like. I would learn and learn and learn and learn, believing that LEARNING ABOUT humans was the only thing to do. Like the cliche autistic boy who learns everything he possibly can about model trains, I learned everything I possibly could ABOUT humans. But it was odd. This time in my life. The first twenty-some odd years of life. Because during this time, even though I was knowledgeable of humans, their stories, and on and on... I didn't sense the humans. I didn't feel connected to the humans. And they, the humans, seemed so bizarre to me... for evidence of this, look no further than the way in which I referred to them as "the humans", as though I was not one.

This overall sense of disconnection and tone-deafness made my pre-LSD life seem very, very strenuous at times. That said, I would also add that these struggles, however unpleasant, did indeed force me to strengthen other aspects of my processing, making me very adept at building complex designs and structures within my mind — e.g., conceptualizing user interfaces, restructuring workflows, and writing lengthy yet (hopefully!) cohesive metaphorical explanations of my LSD-induced shifts in perception. So before we talk in more detail about how LSD has taught me and enabled me, I'd like to talk a bit more about the advantages of perceiving the world as an autistic individual.

One perceived benefit of autistic processing involves the ways in which my narrowed vision and social blindness results in a fair degree of non-reactivity, which in turn makes me especially well-suited to endure the emotional traumas of others, or to quickly arrive at pragmatic solutions in the face of what others might perceive as emotional chaos. Also, although my socially withdrawn state resulted in a lot of intentional isolation, I would also argue that it is this exact type of isolation that made me very well suited for immersive creative processes such as writing and designing books like the one you're reading now :)

And so without further delay, I would like to now tell you the story of what it was like to experience LSD, as an autistic adult, for the very first time.

CHAPTER TWO

AUTISM ON ACID

When I was in my teens, and even in my early 20s, the only thing I could think to do was figure out how the game of being human worked. I'd try to do better next time, over and over again. But the people in my life kept being disappointed. They kept wondering what was wrong with me. And I wondered, too. And let me tell you, if you spend a lot of time wondering what's wrong with you, the odds are incredibly high that you will likewise do nothing but reinforce the belief that something IS wrong with you, and you will probably become very, very depressed in the process.

And I was. I acted very, very depressed. And the most bizarre part of my depression was that I didn't "feel depressed." I felt like sleeping a lot, sure. I felt like staying in my room a lot, sure. I felt like reading books and staying away from the humans, usually. Sure. But I didn't "feel" depressed. I was more so just, lost. So lost. And no one seemed to know where I should go. They weren't me. So how should they know? But I didn't know me. So I tried to rely on them to tell me how I should feel. I let people steer me anywhere, because I had no compass. And it was exhausting.

As the years went by, my social ineptitude left me feeling like there was no point, really. It was a noble effort I'd made, this whole trying to understand human beings thing. Really. I would read psychology books. I would read behavior theories. I would participate in professional psychoanalysis and talk therapy. Tons of it. But that was just more talking with no emotional processing. I would talk to the therapist about philosophy or science, or the news. But the feelings, they just, couldn't be found nor identified. So we talked and talked and talked and therapist after therapist would say the same thing to my parents, "Your son is incredibly bright," they would say. "He must read a lot," they would say. Great. Awesome. Wonderful. Cool. I could get straight A's. But I didn't care all that much about that. Memorizing things and repeating them back was easy. Interpreting human behavior. Good luck!

And so time continued to tick. I graduated college, and entered the workforce, but the core of my condition continued to bewilder me. All I could do was try and try and try to use my head to do what my heart, just, couldn't seem to do. So I visited doctor after doctor, trying medications for depression, and anxiety, and only ever feeling more numb as a result. This one made me sleepy. This one made me spacy. This one made me agitated. This one required that I take this other one, and this other one to deal with the side effects of the first one. It seemed to be a mess, and given my overall sense of satisfaction with being alive to begin with, it surely didn't seem all that worth it to perfect this highly distressing dance of psychiatric trial and error, after error, after error.

For years, it seemed like the nightmare of day-to-day life would never let up. From the vantage point of others, I seemed to be doing alright. But from my own perspective, there hardly seemed to be a point to any of it. So much confusion for seemingly no reward. What was the point?

Amidst these adult years of fatigue and confusion, I was fortunate enough to have decent healthcare through my job and amazing support and guidance from my family. I was also fortunate enough to be able to find a new specialist who provided me with some degree of relief.

He was the psychiatrist I had been seeing for some time. I was 23 years of age, working a 9 to 5 job. And I was anxious, all the time anxious. I had a well-paying career, a studio apartment downtown, and a compassionate and caring girlfriend. And I seemed to have all of the pieces that would complete a life. But there remained a sense of emptiness. I didn't talk about it much, with anyone other than the professionals paid to listen. But I was depressed, very depressed. And my therapist at the time — a rare modern-day hybrid of a psychoanalyst, who could engage in talk therapy, and a psychiatrist, who could prescribe medications — was in a unique position to observe my behaviors through a more well-rounded lens.

During my visits to this therapist's office, I would talk about how, in spite of my exhausting mental state, I remained relatively functional in my job setting, which mainly required me to be on the computer, all day everyday.

I would talk about how I struggled to maintain contact with supposed close friends, and how I struggled to make new friends, and how even one-on-one moments felt very confusing at times. I was physically close to people, but still very much emotionally distant, from others, myself, and really, everyone in my life. I explained how my version of connecting with people was watching TV near them, or playing sports with them. And I explained how this way of socializing seemed passable, but ultimately resulted in a perpetual sense of disconnection.

Time went on and I continued unpacking my social struggles during my visits to the therapist. I explained in more depth about how I felt so overwhelmed in most social settings. I unpacked how my perpetually anxious state made everyday a silent struggle known only by me, and maybe my parents, during the most extreme moments of my life. But all throughout my visits to this therapist's office the emotional undercurrent of my life remained out of reach.

My therapist and I explored some more, talking week after week, never really making any significant progress. I'd feel relieved that someone knew about my struggle, but I didn't seem to know anything else aside from the struggle itself. I was jumping between various medications that seemed to only make me more sluggish, and numb, without any perceived benefit. I wanted to be happy (?) but I didn't seem to know what that meant to begin with. I wanted to be... ? I really didn't know. I just knew that I felt wrong, so wrong. I was convinced I was doing it all wrong. And I just, didn't, know. WHY.

And then one day, when I walked into the therapist's office, he said, "I'd like you to fill this out. It's only a few questions, and shouldn't take you long." And I said, "Okay."

He didn't tell me explicitly at the start of the exam, but what he had handed me was the Autism-Spectrum Quotient (AQ) test. The test itself took only a few minutes. And the therapist was able to score it right then and there. And there it was: 44 out of a possible 50, a very high AQ indicating a dominating presence of autistic traits.

"You're on the spectrum; very high on the spectrum in fact," he said.

"Oh," I said, not so sure of what to say at first.

"Don't worry, it's not the end of the world. It's the start of self-understanding. Here's a few books to read. Check 'em out and we'll talk some more next week."

And I did. I went home and read everything I possibly could about ASD. And with every page I read, my whole life seemed to make more and more and more sense. This was exciting!...

.....to a degree :/

There was a comfort in knowing that I wasn't alone; that others were like me, too. But in time, this intellectual excitement wore off. And there I was again: still numb, still broken, still fumbling around trying to hear the dog whistle that every other dog already hears.

Once again, I would say without a doubt that receiving this diagnosis was of great benefit. Yes, but the diagnosis itself didn't seem to change much about my sense of being tired, so tired. So tired of attempting to connect but so often missing the mark. So tired of attempting to do the seemingly impossible; as in, sensing and identifying and navigating my feelings, or the feelings of others. It was a fool's errand. I couldn't do it. I wouldn't do it. And I began to fully believe I would never ever do it. And that's when one of the darkest thoughts began to take over my mind; the one I'd tried to push away for so long — this idea that I was broken, forever. And that thought was reeeeally starting to get to me. It's a thought that I'm sure any person who's been labeled as disorderly or handicapped or mentally ill can relate to, a lot.

Even years into therapy, I was still coming up against this very dark thought that I was broken, so broken. And I began ruminating on how there wasn't much of a point of going on in this life. No one would miss me. They were strangers anyway. All of them. They all felt like strangers. All of the humans. They were strangers. Even myself. What was I doing here? Why? Why? Why?

I kept going to therapy. I kept reading books. I kept working at my desk job. I kept trying new medications. I kept failing, time and time again, with the simple act of identifying the emotional needs of myself and others. And this pervasive shortcoming kept me in the same old loop. I would feel lost, confused, and isolate myself, and miss calls, and sleep for days. My close connections couldn't and wouldn't put up with it anymore. I faded into a quiet pocket of solitude. I seemed to only be able to be alone. And a lot of connections ended. And then I quit my job. And then my very good friend got struck and killed by a drunk driver. And this series of rapid-fire tragedies seemed to do nothing but confirm in me that life was hell, absolute hell. And nothing I could or would do was going to change that belief. Life was hell. This was hell. And there was no escaping it. That was really how I seemed to believe my life would go. And I was so, so exhausted by that belief.

I dwelled in this sunken state of mind for a long while after my friend's funeral. I would still see people, and do things, but I couldn't shake the deep, deep, deep depressive state. And it seemed to be a never ending loop of negative thoughts... "I'm never going to understand this. I'm never going to figure this out. I'm never going to understand that. I'm never going to do this or anything right." And then, I just couldn't take it anymore.

At that time, living seemed like a waste of energy. It was as if there was nothing and no one worth living for — except for maybe two people: my parents. They had put in so much effort, at so many points in my life, that it just didn't seem fair to them. They'd done so much for me, and I just, couldn't, do it. I wouldn't do it. So I carried on, barely living but at least, living. And on one of the darkest hours of the darkest days, after waking up again, hungover, in my bed, without a friend to phone or a sense of purpose or hope to hold onto, I decided that rather than ending my life, I would instead put an end to the life I had built. And I did what a lot of anxious and confused people do when they're pushed to the limit: I ran away. I went into retreat.

I didn't tell very many people other than the few connections I'd barely managed to maintain in spite of my isolated state. But I retreated. I sold all my stuff. I packed a bag. I bought a train ticket. And I headed west, to see if there was something, anything, that might be worth living for. And a few days into my travels, I was presented with the option to try LSD. And being at a point in my life where I felt very much out of options, I took it. And I sat in a forest, waiting to experience one more failed attempt at escaping the waking hell of existence when suddenly...

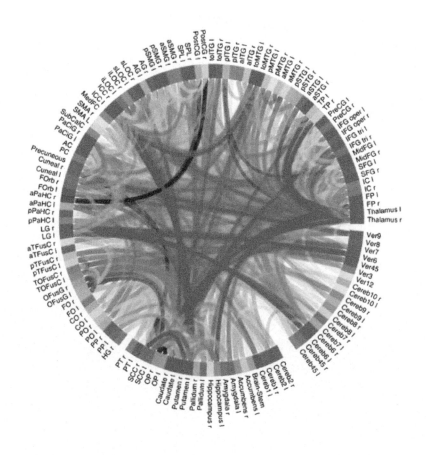

This connectome ring shows functional connectivity between
132 regions covering the whole brain
during LSD exposure.

—

PURE BLACK LINES indicate decreased connectivity
ALL OTHER SHADES OF GREY indicate increased connectivity

—

Figure provided by F. Mueller
Basel fMRI study

—

...said another way...

HOLY.

SHIT!

Connection. Such connection. I felt it, in so many ways. I felt it. And with so many parts of my processing centers woven together for the very first time, so many realizations seemed to come crashing in, all at once.

As it often seems to go with LSD, my first experience felt deeply meaningful to me in the moment and beyond. That day, I took a relatively large dose — the exact amount is unknown but I was told the single tab I took was blotted with between 150 and 250 micrograms of LSD. And while yes, this dose exposed me to many of the commonly described hallmarks of the larger-dose LSD experience, it was what happened after the peak effect that really blew my mind, or should I say, heart, into a state of absolute wonderment.

In the initial hours of the experience, as the LSD began to take effect, I felt more and more connected... with the trees and breeze and sunlight around me. I experienced a deep moment of engagement. Yes. A moment of connection, with nature, with thoughts of my parents, my family, friends, and the whole of the human family and the broader web of life. And yes I know it sounds cliche to say but I was awash in a sense of deep, deep love for so many aspects of life.

This single session with LSD not only washed away the background hum of suicidal ideation but also, amazingly, befuddlingly, wow, what the f*ck! wow! I not only didn't feel like killing myself. I felt very much like living. Because I felt very much alive, and connected. And feeling connected meant I cared about who and what I was connected to. And I felt this sense of connection, deeply. And it wasn't a hallucination. It was a realization. An intuitive sense that my well-being was directly connected to the health and well-being of the natural environment within which I resided.

Expounding on this further, I would say that during the initial hours of my first LSD experience, I felt a sense of care, for myself; for others; for the world. I cared about it, All of it. And I felt like the world of human beings cared about me, too. And it's wonderful, really. To feel like caring; to feel cared for, as well. It's beautiful, really, to feel like I've been nurtured by nature; to feel like it is in my nature to nurture; to nurture myself, others, and the environment in which we attempt to co-exist. But I'm starting to sound like someone who took a lot of acid ;) ... So let me step back down outta the clouds of love for a second and talk about something that some of us might not be as experienced with: the subjective experience of taking LSD as an autistic adult.

After my first few hours of bathing in the wonderment of love for the natural world, I stood up, calmly, and with a deep warmth within me, I walked out of the woods in which I'd been sitting, and I walked down a path, and I turned to the right, and I encountered a stranger. A stranger, yes, that suddenly, somehow, didn't seem strange at all. And I said "Hi." And they said "Hi." And it felt...natural?! I felt...compelled, to connect! And that might not seem like that big of a deal, but for me, it was everything! This type of spontaneous, extroverted encounter was not common in my daily life, most especially amidst my most depressed days. And while yeah, we talked about nothing of tremendous significance, in terms of topics, my heart still lit up as I became aware of how aware I had become.

This experience felt like being a kid riding a bike for the first time. Every time before the first time, the kid can't do it. But then, the kid is doing it. And for a short while, during the first ride, the kid almost doesn't even notice or believe he's doing it. But then, he notices. And it sets in: the kid is doing it! The kid is riding the bike! And it was amazing!

When the person opposite me spoke, I felt the weight of their words. I sensed their state of mind. I grasped the context of what was unfolding. And for the first time in my entire 27 years of existence, I felt fully connected to the person opposite me. I could feel their feelings. I could feel my own feelings. I could feel what it was like to feel differently about my feelings as our feelings changed in real time. I could feel how it felt to feel aware of my own emotions; how it felt to feel aware of my impact on the emotional experience of the person across from me. And again: HOLY SH%T. After this exchange, I walked back to the forest, sat down, and thought "HOLY SH%T! What just happened! I've never done that before. I've talked to people. Sure. But I've never talked WITH a person like that. The nuance. The detail. The richness of the exchange."

This particular interaction seemed like the difference between scarfing down a meal versus contemplating and savoring the taste of every bite. Every little detail mattered, and every little detail gave me that much more information to work with. I didn't have to follow the script of "Hi, how are you, good, how are you, good, ok, great"... It was more than that. This exchange. I saw new opportunities to notice what the person was really saying. What they desired. What pained them. What delighted them. I could see it in such detail. And I could interact with them with a careful approach.

Again, pardon my language here. I really don't have an adequate phrase for how powerful this experience felt. So HOLY SH%T seems like a good place holder for the time being. Because yes, HOLY SH%T! This thing I'd never been able to do... I could do it. I wasn't locked inside the observation bubble. I was out there, interacting with the world; interacting with people with an unprecedented amount of mental dexterity and deeply felt, empathetic processing. And sure. Yes. I had interacted with people before, but never like this; never with such a deep and wide-reaching awareness of what was unfolding.

In the past I would lean on memorized lines or just try my best to answer the questions proposed to me. But in this exchange, when I heard a question, I not only considered what answer to give. I was able to consider how the phrasing of my answer might alter the tone of the engagement, and how any given verbal or non-verbal response might change the directionality of the exchange. It wasn't just an if-this-phrase-then-this-response kind of thing. It was more like because-this-sensation-you-can-say-this-or-do-this-or-that-and--that-will-alter-this-and-that-sensation-in-you-and-in-the-other-person-so-observe-and-sense-and-interact-however-feels-right kind of thing... In other words: I could be delicate, with my words and actions. And I could be conscious of the impact of my words and movements, because I felt their weight, within myself, within the person across from me. Empathy. Arresting empathy. I felt it. And HOLY SH%T did this newly available emotional empathetic processing seem like a useful and meaningful aspect of conscious experience.

So yes, that was my first experience. And so perhaps now you can see why it is that I persisted in my exploration of the intersection of LSD and ASD. Because LSD was the turnkey for my life. LSD simultaneously saved my life while at the same time imbuing it with a sense of meaning, connection, and accessibility. And it was thrilling. Yes. But before I continue on with the story of what occurred after that first experience, I would like to take a moment to calm us down.

So yes, let's all calm down.

Because YES, absolutely, YES, this experience was profoundly impactful on me. YES. But I would like to calmly say to both myself, the writer, and to you, the reader, that even though this experience was especially significant, I still find it critical to voice a word of caution regarding everything I'm talking about.

First of all: this type of experience of unity and connection seems to be common in the LSD experiences of many people, as evidenced by both numerous subjective accounts as well as published accounts from various research studies. So this unity aspect, however amazing it may be for the individual, isn't all that remarkable in terms of progressing the cultural and scientific understanding of the potential applications for LSD.

Second of all: in reference to the dramatic empathetic increase I experienced, I've likewise since learned, after digging into the established research of LSD, that this property is likewise not as much of a miracle as it seemed to be at the time. Based on what I've read, it seems like this type of empathetic experience is probably more so just a boring old combination of (1) direct stimulation of the 5-HT2A receptors

(2) key fluctuations in amygdalic response, (3) adequate suppression of the default mode network, and (4) a corresponding increase in between-brain-region connectivity that I would absolutely need like a decade of schooling or someone with an actual PhD to possibly ever explain. And speaking of doctors, I'm still not one, yet. But I can still advise some caution. So here we go...

Let's start with the hopefully obvious point: LSD is still an unregulated and illegal drug. So anyone who hears of my story, please, please, please, for the sake of your own safety and the safety of others, please do not consider this story to be an invitation to try this at home. This epiphany happened within me. And that's great. But I'm not here to recommend that anyone repeat my exact actions. There are risks inherent to any frontier exploration of this kind, most especially when it comes to experimenting with unregulated materials that could be impure, or obtained with only vague certainty of the exact amount of a given dose.

In the early phase of this process, I took on the risks because I felt out of options. In the later phases, I took on the risks because the gains felt worthwhile, to me and my sense of self-understanding. But that doesn't mean I'm wise for persisting in my self-experimentation. There could be longterm side effects to routine LSD use that we don't yet know about. And that makes sense given the prohibition-driven drought of longitudinal studies — which, again, is why I'm advocating for a rescheduling and rethinking of access for the purposes of research.

If the research continues to support phenomenological reports with measurable evidence and efficacy, then sure, yes, let's rethink some approaches. And maybe in a decade we can open up LSD-assisted therapy centers for sociocognitive deficits. And I hope we can, because drugs such as LSD or psilocybin or MDMA seem like excellent candidates for increasing the impact of already well-established approaches to therapy. But we're not fully there yet. And so, out of respect for the benefits and necessity of proper research, proper regulation, and proper professional guidance, I repeat: don't try this at home. But maybe, someday, try this under the supervision of trained and certified professionals.

But I digress. Let's get back to the story. Where were we? Ah yes, I was just about to tell you what happened AFTER my first LSD experience.

CHAPTER THREE

AFTER THE FIRST DOSE

In the days after my first LSD experience, I fell into a state of necessary reflection. Something deeply impactful had happened to me that day. LSD had not only obliterated all thoughts of suicide. It had also given me a tremendous sense of enablement. I could do something totally new. I could live my life in a totally new way. I was like a deaf person who'd received a cochlear implant. I could hear new tones. I could see new cues. I could readily feel feelings, and identify feelings. And it was thrilling.... but still...... a bit... awkard, not only in terms of it being a bit strange to use the new tools, as though I was an amputee acclimating to their new animatronic arm. But also in the sense of it being awkward because my animatronic arm of polytropic empathy was suddenly in touch with some rather challenging and intense emotions.

In the weeks and months that followed my first LSD experience, I continued to explore the world through the lens of LSD, intentionally placing myself in very low-risk settings, and equipping myself with a great deal of information regarding precautions, interactions, and behavioral therapy approaches in order to make any sort of noteworthy progress.

During my early self-experimentation period with LSD, there were all sorts of newly sensible stimuli to explore. And that was awesome. Sure. But again: challenges still arose, often. Some of the new download of stimulus included the sudden sensing of deep sadness, regret, shame, guilt, on and on. It was as if LSD had unclogged a lifetime of emotional constipation, and there I was, sifting through my mound of unprocessed mental sh*t. But the odd part about this was that, with the assistance of LSD, this type of inner emotional work seemed not very burdensome. Again, it's odd. Because you'd think that processing sadness would make me sad. But it didn't. It made me a bit fatigued at times, yes. And yes, I would cry at times. But all of this ultimately only made me more aware. And with the aid of LSD, I began growing through "aha!" moment after "aha!" moment, seeing my choices and behaviors through a totally new and utile lens.

As I continued to reflect, and work through my issues with LSD present in my system, I developed a new relationship with feelings in general. I went from thinking that feelings were good or bad to thinking that feelings were... useful, insightful, informative, actionable. Supposedly negative emotions didn't seem to be a curse at all. Feeling feelings — good, bad, or otherwise — meant that I could make necessary changes in my life. And with continuous access to these feelings came the intuitive understanding that life was far more nuanced than I could have ever imagined. It was ups and downs. It was expectations met and unmet. It was so many things. And because I could sense the weight of all of this through the lens of LSD, I could likewise look back, and forward, and make sense of the hedge maze of being alive as an autistic individual, and also, as just, a person, with a set of circumstances, and differences, just like any other person. And so it was also through this process that I experienced an uptick in appreciation for the struggles and strength of so many people in my life, including my parents, my friends, and yes, myself.

I saw myself as a survivor. And as I looked back at those darkest hours of those darkest days, I looked lovingly upon myself, almost as if I was noticing the behaviors of a frightened child. Even the person who I seemed to be just a year prior. That identity, and that way of being, seemed childlike somehow.

I didn't realize it during my first few LSD experiences — because I was very much preoccupied trying out all the new features at first — but through enough reflection, I came to realize how my autistic processing impacted every other aspect of my anxiety-riddled social existence. The low-fidelity nature of my pre-LSD sensory processing contributed to my generally aloof state in so many small but pervasive ways. I was the last to realize so many things in a given social exchange. I was just, stuck, inside, myself. And while stuck inside, I didn't seem to have the slightest clue about the temperatures of my heart, or the temperatures of the hearts around me, so to speak. And this hyposensitivity seemed to be a global symptom that extended beyond my touch-based emotional sensitivity into my more run-of-the-mill touch-based senses.

Often, in my pre-LSD life, I would fail to sense fluctuations in the actual temperature, as in literally, hot and cold environments, and that also made people look at me sideways. It's odd, really, to have interruptions in the sensory feedback loop. I would dress with thin layers in winter all the time, and other people were often the first to let me know that my body was probably cold, even if I, the observer, hadn't yet realized it. In this way, as a child, I would often rely on my parents or others to serve as a sort of external awareness alarm for me. And that was just one more small but significant challenge preventing me from confidently navigating the world as an independent autistic adult.

And so as I continued to look back from the newly available vantage point of these early LSD experiences, I saw how all of my hyposensitivity, and aloofness, and being slow on the uptake.... in my pre-LSD life... made me want to just, isolate myself, from everybody. But as I continued working with LSD present in my system, I seemed to be increasingly capable of perceiving how others might have seen me — as in me, little boy Aaron, before LSD — and I gained a sort of empathy for who and how I used to be.

I looked back and relived moments of public disorientation, meltdown, and fatigue. I likewise revisited the perpetual sense of hopelessness I seemed to used to feel at the end of most days. And I understood it. I understood and forgave myself for not perceiving critical stimuli that my brain seemed to either ignore or simply not pick up on at all. And it's odd. Because as soon as I seemed to be able to perceive these new subsets of seemingly more relevant stimuli, I could then rapidly overlay a given "aha!" moment over previous experiences, and run the mental math I had left undone during the initial exchange. Like "Ohhhhh so that's why they said that...Ohhhh that's how what I did that one time must have impacted the other person ..... Ohhhhh they meant that, even though they said that.... Ohhhhhh, wow."

All the dots seemed to connect. Like a kid being shown how the magic trick is done, I was a kid that got a glimpse of how the mind performs the magic of perception. And it changed my view of the show. I could pick up on subtler cues, and see new angles on seemingly routine behaviors. And this ability to see more than the typically summarized view of the world afforded me the ability to likewise build more well-rounded views of what people in my life were feeling, desiring, and communicating to me in ways other than words.

By contrast, prior to my first LSD experience, I felt connected to knowledge, but not much else. I was full of factoids and stories and dates and explanations and on and on and on, but I was empty, emotionally. And then, LSD. And then, feeling feelings and noticing emotionally charged patterns embedded in social behavior, body language, and other non-verbal cues. These bits of data became a whole new dimensions of experience, and the insights seemed to add up so quickly, both in terms of my ability to process them as well as the total quantity of "aha!" moments I seemed to be able to experience in the early phases of my immersion with LSD.

And there I was, a 27-year old kid in an emotional candy store, sampling all of the feelings. I would take small to medium doses of LSD and watch and rewatch movies from my youth and be SHOCKED to start crying or want to cheer for the protagonist and WOWED when I would imagine that perhaps that is what other people experience all of the time. Maybe "neurotypical" or "typically developing" people watch a movie and feel things deeply, too? I didn't do that. If someone started to cry in front of me when I was growing up, I would sorta just, stand there, the same way I might stand around awkwardly if I'd spill a fountain soda in a fast food restaurant, and I'd want to help clean it up, but the staff had the only mop and insisted upon cleaning it up, so they did, but I still felt weird and awkward so I'd stand there, acting strange. And that was me, time after time, when deeply emotional moments arose in others, I would say something like "Don't cry! Crying is bad! Eat ice cream!", because I didn't know how to deal with the emotional complexity of others. So generally, I avoided such encounters, or I made my best guess at mimicking what actors did in movies when other people became distressed. But either way, I didn't get it.

Before LSD, emotionality was an invisible phenomenon; a frequency that didn't register on the radio transceiver of my heart and mind. But then, LSD. And then, feeling feelings, processing feelings, working through feelings, performing emotional labor. It was all very new but also very knowable. And thus began the process of integrating my insights into my daily life.

CHAPTER FOUR

INTEGRATION

In the case of partially colorblind individuals, there exists specialized eyeglasses that help the wearer to differentiate between otherwise ambiguous, or, overlapping tones of color. In the case of my ASD-affected perceptions, LSD seemed to work similarly on the tonalities of emotion, the clarity of social cues, and in turn, the depth and abundance of perceivable salient stimuli to which I could react. As I said in the intro of this essay, LSD sharpened my view by separating out the sensory information in such a way that it was not only more sensible, but also more workable, readable, and navigable. Even so, the early phase of traversing this learning curve wasn't always pleasant.

Feeling feelings so deeply was a profound experience. Yes. But feeling the depth of sadness, or the intense pain of loss, became, as I said earlier, a challenge of a different sort. So yes, LSD helped me access empathetic processing. But a lot of that emotional exploration brought me face to face with some rather unsavory moments in my life; the innumerable memories of times when I wasn't accessible, emotionally, to myself, to other people. And the intuitive, felt realization that I had been the cause of emotional pain in others, in turn, forced me to experience a great deal of delayed, deep pain, within myself, too.

Once again... I remind you that my ASD didn't meet LSD until I was 27. And that means that I'd lived an entire 27 years without access to this depth of emotional and social sensory processing. So naturally, once I gained direct and deeply felt access to this type of sensory experience, I had a lot of reflecting to do. I was like a deaf person who finally got their cochlear implant — that which was once silent became suddenly sensible. And even though the initial breakthrough into empathetic processing was a joyous moment overall, that's not to say it didn't also come with a whole lot of thinking to myself "Man, I must have looked like such a jerk. Man, I must have sounded so insensitive." And yes, that hurt. It hurt to realize how much emotional pain could hurt. But at least this feeling of hurt, and shame, and regret, gave me something to work with; something to use to formulate a plan for improvement. Because once I could feel these negative states so strongly and readily, I could likewise feel the urge to adjust patterns of behavior accordingly. And so began years of working through my behaviors, past and present, little by little, with the assistance of LSD.

I looked backwards at countless moments in my life; countless times in which the person opposite me was undergoing an intense emotional experience as I sat by, guessing at what was... wrong? Guessing at what I did or what I should do or ummm, yeah I don't know how to explain it... I just didn't know what they were going through. They seemed to have been stabbed but there was no knife present. So what was the odd behavior all about? I would say I was sorry they were feeling how they were feeling but in truth I didn't know how they were feeling. I didn't know. I didn't know. I didn't know. And that was my whole issue: I was trying to KNOW the feeling, through rationality and deduction. But in order to FEEL the feeling, I would have had to have experienced the feeling. And I didn't. I hadn't. I hadn't experienced the feeling. Whatever feeling they were feeling, I didn't feel it. I couldn't sense it. I cried when I fell and broke my bones. Sure. But these other kinds of cryings were very, very odd to me.

As I previously mentioned in this text, my younger self would learn the dance steps of life via rote memorization. Adults would explain the steps to me. They'd say "Hey say thank you after this happens. Don't do this. Don't do that. If someone does this, do this." On and on. And I made mental notes and leaned on these kinds of if-this-then-that flowcharts to survive in a totally foreign landscape of hard-to-see signals.

The perceptual experience of ASD is the most bizarre thing to try to describe to someone who's not on the spectrum, because from the vantage point of others, on the outside, it looks like regular old life unfolding. People talked at me. I'd talk at them. But I still didn't "get it", whatever "it" was. I didn't get it. I didn't get the point. I was just, surviving; walking through a blizzard-like barrage of foreign signals; signals that were inherently foreign because they weren't yet perceivable. But again, it's very odd. Because there's this odd imbalance between the amount of stimulus received versus the amount of stimulus processed properly. Like, I would see a lot of the puzzle pieces of social interaction. But when I tried to put them together to prove I'd been paying attention, the person opposite me would be like "Ummm... what? Were you even paying attention?" But that's the funny thing. I was paying attention, as best as I could. But I was paying attention to the seemingly irrelevant stimuli. And to compound the situation, my brain seemed to only ever fluctuate between being overwhelmed or frozen, as though the emergency shut-off was being triggered over and over and over in the face of the trauma of basic social exchanges.

The closest I can come to describing what it's like to have an ASD-affected brain would be to compare it to relying on a mailroom clerk who receives all of the envelopes in the mail but only ever seems to have no clue as to which envelopes ought to be opened first. Based on the research I've done exploring numerous unifying theories of autistic processing and the neural correlates of the LSD experience, I'm inclined to believe this sociocognitive deficit might be rooted in the potentially abnormal functioning of my default mode network, and the correlative low functional connectivity in terms of between-brain network crosstalk. But we'll get to the scientific wonderings later along in this text. For now, let's stick to the biographic espousings.

As I was saying: Before LSD, I could talk about facts, and categories of information, and dates and persons and concepts of all sorts. But when it came down to connecting with myself, or others, on an emotional level, I just... couldn't. I would completely miss the point, and miss the context of what someone was saying. I would hear the words. I would see their face move. And then I'd put it together, bit by bit, and be like "Here's my best attempt at relating to you!" and they'd be like "ummm what?"... And this was my life. Playing the same dumb game over and over. And sure, with enough failures, I learned some patterns of behavior that seemed to... work? But they were guesses. And yes, we all guess. But my guesses seemed to be way off, way often.

Yes, I had some friendships anchored by shared enjoyment of sports or movies or ideas of all sorts. But socializing with new people or in large groups was most often avoided for the simple reason that it was exhausting. And I didn't seem to be very good at it. And I relate this to the feeling that an armless man would feel being invited to play pitcher at the baseball game. Sure, I could show up. But I'd rather skip the part where I fail, again and again and again, and just stay at home, and read in my room. So I did.

More often than not, I put socializing as the very last priority on my list. And this isn't a tragedy in and of itself. There's plenty of pleased introverts in the world. And at times, I too found satisfaction in the creative projects I'd made, by myself, in my inner world. But it was probably confusing for other people, who wondered why I would leave early, or not show up at all. And there were so many moments with people who were close to me in my life who then had to be confronted with this sense that I didn't seem to notice their emotional needs. And I would fall out of touch so often. I was unresponsive for long periods of time. I would hide in my room. I would play it safe, opting for computer screens and books versus people and parties, which again, is totally fine! But there were still days when it seemed very obvious to me that ideas and information alone couldn't nourish me; that there was more to life than rote memorization.

And that's where LSD was the most assistive to me in my life, giving me the lens I needed to fear less, see more, and connect with the people in my life in an intensely meaningful way.

And for all the ways that LSD helped me feel this deep sense of connection, perhaps the most important and deep connection of all was the one I reformed with myself.

CHAPTER FIVE

ACCEPTANCE

Although the very simplified version of my essay is "LSD gave me the 'neurological contact lenses' I needed to sense emotionality and feel connected to others"... the slightly more nuanced version of this summary would also include the part where the increased sensory awareness also allowed me to reconnect with myself as an autistic individual. Because as a result of my early LSD explorations, I likewise became my own best friend after a long period of self-rejection. In other words: as my overall outlook and relationship toward my perceptions continued to shift, I likewise began seeing my autistic perception as just another lens.

Some of us are colorblind. Some of us are not. Some of us are autistic. Some are not. This is Neurodiversity 101: Don't judge a fish by its ability to climb a tree. Great. Got it.

The reason I bring this up is: we all seem to have unique lenses through which we experience the world. The interesting twist on this however seems to be that in my case, the addition of LSD to my life allowed me to not only change lenses, but also, to be able to change BETWEEN lenses, back and forth. It was a bit like the eye doctor asking, which one is more clear, "Number 1? Number 2? Number 1? Number 2? LSD? ASD? LSD? ASD?"

By alternating between the lenses of ASD and LSD, I gained an intimate understanding of not only a new way of seeing, but also, critically, a wholly new and novel perspective on the ways that I had always seen. I became aware of the ways in which I was aware, and unaware, of various aspects of the ever-available stimulus. In this way, I became capable of seeing my own biases, and conditioned patterns of belief, and so many other aspects of self that had become so familiar and ingrained that they had likewise become more or less invisible to me in my day-to-day perception. And I became better able to see how I see, so to speak. And in this way, LSD gave me the new eyes I needed to see my old eyes in new ways, and to appreciate them, likewise.

I have intentionally worn the lens of LSD in moments requiring immense emotional labor. I have intentionally gone without the lens of LSD for long portions of time, most especially during periods in which I sought to explore my ASD tendencies from a more direct vantage point. And this fluidity of intelligence; this timely use of different lenses, seems to work well for me. Because again: one lens isn't necessarily better than the other. Just. Different. And that's what I've come to experience, directly, by changing between the lenses of ASD and LSD.

All of this is just a fancy bit of wordplay but to put it another way: I can choose to wear the lenses of introvertedness, or extrovertedness. I can retreat into the turtle shell of my muted, lo-fi ASD perspective, or open up the blinds and experience the hi-fi LSD perspective. Culturally, we do this all of the time, whether it's with a mind-churning cup of coffee or a mind-quieting glass of wine. But again, when it comes to managing the abnormal functional connectivity of ASD, LSD seems to be much more valuable than a mere stimulant or depressant. Because for me, LSD serves as a reliable entactogen (a term coined by Metzner and Nichols in 1983; a term derived from the roots "en" [within], "tactus" [touch], "gen" [produce]). And the entactogenic property of LSD is a critical drug effect I didn't know I needed.

Up until the day I met LSD, I was trying to take other medicines to be happy (?), not even realizing that what I needed the most was to FEEL and IDENTIFY happiness, and also unhappiness, and also anger, and on and on and on. Because as I've progressed through this type of inner work, it seems to be the case that in order to heal, I need to feel. In order to shed the weight of anxiousness and dawn the robe of acceptance, I have come to know the knowledge and feel the feelings I might be afraid to know and feel. And LSD helps me to approach the intentional act of inner exploration with a lessened sense of fear. And this same fear-lowering effect has been reported and measured in studies exploring the neuropharmacologic properties of MDMA, but that's a story for another day.

Thanks to LSD, I've become capable of walking between two worlds: the highly "mental" worldview of ASD processing and the "mind-body" worldview made possible by a presumed increase in overall functional connectivity. And that's the rationale for the subtitle of this essay "Autism on Acid: How LSD Helped Me Bridge The ASD-Neurotypical Divide".... Because LSD didn't "rescue me" from autism. It showed me an alternative to autistic perception. And by being able to select my preferred mode of operation, I feel enabled in the sense that I can choose to wear a particular lens for a particular environment, challenge, or situation. And I am grateful to have the ability to choose between these various vantage points of conscious experience, because it is a significant upgrade from being locked inside one vantage point and mode of perception.

Not all deaf people want cochlear implants. But at least, we give them a choice. If we have a means of improving their quality of life, we at least offer it to them as an option. In my view, access to medicines such as LSD seem to be of similar importance to the individuals who are impaired in other ways.

Metaphorically speaking, experiencing the sudden onset of emotional intuition seemed sorta like if a blind paraplegic man suddenly and simultaneously regained his eyesight AND his sensation in his legs and then realized a rabid dog had been biting his ankle for what looks like years. If his brain wasn't receiving the sensory signals, how could he have noticed? The critical connections were severed, disconnected. And so in this particular metaphor, LSD would be the equivalent of a spinal reattachment; a patching together of my heart and mind, so to speak. Thanks to LSD, I can now come to know when the dog of emotion is biting me. I can identify the sensation. I can make a choice to deal with the sensation. And that means that I can navigate my life in a wholly new way: feeling my way forward. And this might sound like "Oh cool big deal you're in touch with your feelings, cool" but YES, for me this is a huge deal. 27 years of social vertigo and interpersonal confusion damn near killed me. So yes, it is a very big deal. Because in a very real way: LSD saved my life.

Okay, okay. My ASD processing is not and has never been directly life threatening in a purely physiological sense. In terms of being evolutionarily fit for survival, I could see well enough to avoid traffic. I could feel my body well-ish enough to know that I should probably put a jacket on because it's cold... but as I mentioned earlier, even that wasn't always the case... Either way, the point is: even before LSD, I could talk and listen well enough to perform tasks... and that meant I could make money and pay for food and shelter. And that was functional... to a point. But in the days before LSD, I was still demonstrating behaviors of a depressed person on the spectrum, ideating on suicide, avoiding people, acting frustrated, rarely understanding myself and others. And that was me. All of the time, me.

Before LSD, I seemed to be disappointing person after person who seemed to be invalidated by my tone-deafness. Person after person who seemed to be confused about why I was laughing when the story they were explaining wasn't a comedy. Person after person who would go through a terrifically complicated series of facial movements and fidgeting for reasons that I couldn't discover. And that was me, the forensic socializer. Trying to figure out WHY the humans were doing what they were doing. Like, what was the reward? There had to be a reward, right? Why else would they act like that? I truly didn't know.

Thankfully, LSD allowed me to see the matrix of socializing. And over time, LSD also seemed to help me improve my relationships with both myself and other people. And I could've never learned how to act more harmoniously if I'd never gotten the chance to hear and sense the tones of others through the assistance of LSD.

My healing began with a large dose taken at a point of desperation and evolved into smaller doses and specific regimens taken with a high degree of intention. Over time, I developed and refined the approaches that worked for me, and slowly but surely, I learned how to transform the act of socializing from a purely mechanical process into a much more first-nature exchange of feeling.

To accomplish these gains, I leveraged a methodology developed over the course of years of first-hand trial and error. And this approach — an approach I call immersion therapy — seems like something worth sharing with the world, if for no other reason than to inspire therapists and researchers to consider alternate approaches in this already alternate field.

CHAPTER SIX

IMMERSION THERAPY

In order to explain LSD-Assisted Immersion Therapy, it's best that I start by saying what it is not. It is not taking such a high dose that I intend to enter a state of "cosmic unity" (which can be useful for other reasons, in other contexts). And it's also not taking such a small "microdose" that the effect is "subperceptive"... because clearly, the goal of my particular type of immersion therapy is to alter my perception. But here again we come to an issue of linguistics.

This idea of a "mind-altering substance"... it's a bit, wiggly. Generally, the term seems to carry the cultural connotation that the alteration is, for some reason or another, undesired. In my case, however, the alteration was... welcomed. I would intentionally take a "mind-altering substance" that would alter my mind. And this alteration would likewise alter the way in which I would perceive and process a variety of stimuli. This change in perception and processing seems note-worthy and assistive, but not necessarily "good" or "bad". Just, different.

I appreciate the perspective that LSD has given to me, just as I appreciate the perspective that ASD has given to me, too. And it is important for me to point out that although I persisted in my quest to try to learn and understand more about this new mode of perception and processing, I still feel that my previous, ASD-affected processing wasn't exactly "disorderly". Rather, I would consider my ASD-affected processing to be a unique variation of the human experience; a mode of cognition that just so happens to prioritize certain stimuli over other stimuli in a given situation.

And so now we arrive at two key terms: Monotropism, this tendency to focus on a narrow attention tunnel, and Polytropism, the tendency to process multiple inputs simultaneously. Both monotropic and polytropic processing approaches have their advantages and disadvantages. But in the case of autistic individuals, it has been theorized that polytropic processing is perhaps inaccessible or at least, the less dominant method, as opposed to monotropic processing. In my experience, LSD appears to be one such way of inducing a state of polytropic awareness.

Given the marked difference between the experience of monotropic and polytropic processing, I feel that I made a tremendous amount of progress the first time that I took LSD and experienced polytropic processing for the simple reason that I became aware that I *could* experience the world in this other, markedly different way. Polytropic perception wasn't an intellectual idea. It was a lived experience. I felt like a juggler who suddenly grew more limbs. And once I knew that I *could* juggle multiple balls of perceptual input, that was all I needed. From the moment I first experienced this mode of perception, I knew I could learn how to work with it. I trusted I could hone the craft, because LSD gave me the vision. And so began my highly intentional journey toward acclimating myself to polytropic attention, perception, processing, and awareness.

From the very start of this journey, I've embraced the gift of polytropic processing. As a result of this acceptance, I've likewise come to both appreciate and comprehend the particularly intense, multi-sensory empathetic experiences engendered by LSD, more and more, over time. Even so, for however amazing and arresting it may have seemed to be able to see in this new way at first, my progress was still slow at various stages. In the beginning, it took me a long, long while to learn how to use the new features, even if the use of said features seemed to be some sort of intuitive or innate process. It still took practice.

As I stated earlier in this text, the experience of learning how to operate a functionally connected LSD-affected mind seemed a bit like being an amputee acclimating to a new animatronic limb. Challenging, sure. But the reward for learning how to navigate experiences with this new assistive technology seemed to be so significant that the desire to persist in learning seemed to be significant likewise. And in addition to learning *how* to navigate with the lens of LSD, I likewise had to learn *how much* LSD would serve me in a given application.

Over time, and through a great deal of refinement, I found it to be the case that LSD-Assisted Immersion Therapy seemed to work best when I was taking a dose of between 20 and 50 *micro*grams — as in 20 to 50 *MILLIONTHS* of a gram — of LSD. I was working with blotted paper. So to give you an idea of how small of an amount I'm talking about, I would explain it as such: each square paper tab — which measured roughly 5 millimeters wide, 5 millimeters tall, and 1 millimeter thick — contained one 100-microgram drop of liquid LSD. As such, each small square paper tab = ~100 micrograms; half of a tab = ~50 micrograms, and so on. If it's still not clear to you how small of an amount I'm talking about, consider the following visual:

Let's use a one-cent U.S. coin as a frame of reference. If I was to place a 100-microgram square tab of LSD upon a one-cent U.S. coin, the tab would occupy a surface area roughly the size of Abraham Lincoln's head. As such, for therapeutic doses, I was taking an amount that was somewhere between the surface area of Abraham Lincoln's beard (20μg) and the hair on top of his head (50μg), with microdoses (5μg) equating to roughly one of Abe's ears.

Now. In reality I wasn't pulling out a penny to measure the surface area of my blotter dose. Instead, I measured the dose by making a series of diagonal cuts that would in turn result in relatively accurate, or at least, consistent, geometric doses, in a process resembling that of splitting a prescription pill. Using this method, one diagonal cut of a 100-microgram square tab would create two 50-microgram triangles; cut once more and that 50-microgram triangle would become two 25-microgram triangles, and so on and so forth. This measurement method was far from perfect, but at the time, it aligned with the tools I had at my disposal (utility knife, enthusiasm), and the method likewise afforded me the ability to at least make my doses consistent within a given batch of LSD blotter.

LSD Blotter Dose as Compared to Size of a Penny

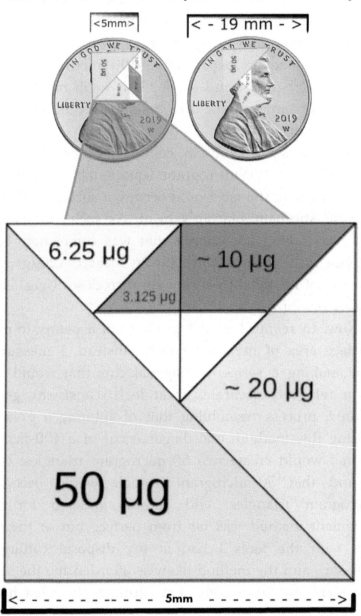

Now, I won't get into it here because the method is a bit more complex than I care to explain right now. But! There are also much more precise volumetric measurement methods made possible with liquid LSD. And these same volumetric methods can also be achieved even with blotter paper. Again, I'm summarizing here but.... Blotter paper blotted with LSD can be placed into a distilled liquid solution that can then be more precisely measured through the use of a medical syringe. In the case of both liquid LSD as well as LSD-blotted paper placed into a distilled solution, the resulting liquid is then absorbed sublingually — as in, squirted under the tongue to be absorbed — in the same way that LSD-blotted paper would be absorbed, as well. But again, I won't say much more than that. If you really want to know more about these methods, do some Googling. And if you really want to be safe, don't do any of this. Seriously.

Once again, I remind us all that — just as the agressively legalese preface to this book indicates — this writing exists for the purpose of entertainment, and the sharing of information, only. This isn't meant to be a "how-to" guide. And I include these specifics simply so that researchers can be aware of my methodology, and not so that someone can mistake me for a doctor and do something unwise or dangerous. But I digress, as I so often do.

In summary: the quantity of LSD I took on immersion days was indeed small in terms of size and weight. Even so, in my experience, there was still a very real and discernible difference between the perceptive effect of taking 50µg versus

25μg, versus 12.5μg versus 6.25μg, etc... and I'll speak a bit about that as we move through this chapter.

So yes. That was how I went about measuring doses in the early phase of my self-guided experimentation. And that was effective...ish. But either way, separate from measuring the dose itself, there was also the task of determining the appropriate dose to take on a given immersion day. To arrive at this amount, I would consider the intended application in terms of the qualities of the anticipated environment as well as the anticipated quantity of familiar or unfamiliar human beings I'd be encountering throughout that immersion day.

The smallest dose I would take on immersion days would be about 20μg, which was a little bit larger than a so-called sub-perceptive dose or microdose (5-15μg), but still significantly smaller than a so-called "large dose" (100μg or more) or "transcendent dose" (250-500μg). Doses of larger magnitude definitely require guidance. And I know I already said it multiple times already but please don't try this at home.

A dose of 20μg, sometimes referred to as a "threshold dose" was the most common dose I would take for the purpose of enabling polytropic processing. The main reason I took this amount, as opposed to larger amounts, was that more than 50μg would engender and induce more pronounced "psychedelic" effects such as audio-visual synesthesia, ego dissolution, astral projection, cosmic unity, etc., all of which could be potentially distracting from the task at hand: social learning and development.

Another key point worth making: with larger doses, there was also an increased likelihood of experiencing the often very pleasant yet occasionally unhelpful side effect of feeling wholly fulfilled by something as simple as the act of admiring a dew-dropped maple leaf sparkling in the afternoon sunlight.

So yes. The general takeaway here is that microdoses (5-15µg), immersion therapy doses (20-50µg), and larger doses (100µg+) all seemed to be useful for specific purposes, in specific settings, with specific intentions. And I say this both based on the first-hand accounts I've read, as well as the first-hand experiences I've lived. From doses large and small, I have grown. But again, don't try this at home!

Some years into my self-experimenting phase of managing my mental health via LSD did indeed include LSD microdosing regimens — for the purpose of SSRI replacement — as well as larger dose one-off experiences for the purpose of taking a deep-dive exploration into the nature of consciousness. Again: all of the aforementioned approaches seemed to yield a benefit, but no single approach was better than the other, much in the same way that a view from the mountaintop yields different insights into the terrain versus the view from basecamp, or halfway up the mountain, etc.

So yes. 20-50 micrograms. It was a variable dose range that seemed to work well for me; a range that would decrease my fear and increase my perceptivity but still allow me to re-root and more readily integrate insights into aspects of selfhood in real time. Because to describe this line of reasoning in another way: if the dose was so large that my sense of selfhood existed in the background rather than foreground of my awareness — as seems to be the case when the default mode network dramatically downregulates during high dose experiences of LSD, or psilocybin, among various other compounds — then it might be difficult to work on matters concerning personal identity, and interpersonal relationships between myself and others.

For the purposes of therapeutic exploration and sociocognitive training, I would take a dose of between 20 and 50 micrograms on a given therapy day, and still maintain adequate washout periods in between sessions. Reason being: LSD has a very particular tolerance profile. And daily use of the drug will not and cannot yield the same effect. As far as research shows, the body needs a few days before tolerance resets to baseline. And so it came to be that I followed a protocol outlined by Dr. James Fadiman.

Following this protocol, I would take a therapeutic dose of LSD every 3 days (dose, off day, off day, dose), always in the morning, and always with a firm idea of my intention and an assured familiarity and comfortability with my setting. Given the occasionally unpredictable nature of these types of experiences, I found it best to also have readily actionable backup plans; a cozy place to go if I needed a lower stimulus environment; a pair of headphones and calm instrumental music, etc.

In a lot of ways, prepping for an LSD experience wasn't all that different from my years of planning ahead for the inevitable need for a low-stimulus environment as an autistic adult. After so many years of feeling so often anxious or inexplicably overwhelmed in various settings, I was very, very skilled at the fine art of situational seclusion.

In regard to set (mindset) and setting (as in, environment), it's important to note that when I would take a therapeutic dose, I would do so with the intention to interface with the world of human beings. I wouldn't put on an eyeblind and headphones and lay down on a couch. I would go into the world of people... on LSD.

Once again, I feel compelled to voice this approach is NOT recommended for anyone new to this type of experience. Guides matter. Therapists and support matter. Because there are a number of seemingly bizarre peripheral phenomena and sensations that may arise during the experience, which means there's likewise a number of potentially challenging outcomes that require extensive planning and risk-mitigating approaches.

So yes, we must prepare. Whenever we are altering our consciousness — whether we are doing so through medicine, breathwork, espresso coffee, ultra-marathons, whatever — we must be prepared.

In planning for these therapeutic dosing days, I took as much precaution as possible through research, and by utilizing the support and guidance of those who had also undergone such experiences in their own lives. And I likewise spoke openly with those close to me so that they could monitor me before, during, and after the experiences, and participate in the feedback loop, from preparation to integration. This same method applied any time I had titrated up or down with prescribed psychiatric medicines in my younger years. When approaching something new, I would inform others in my life of the change, and invite them to assist me in with reflections upon my state of wellbeing as well as the refinement of my overall approach.

As far as dosing was concerned, that wasn't always the easiest at first. When I was first trying to find the dose that worked for me, not only was there the inherently difficult task of titration to deal with, as there would be with any initial use of any psychiatric medicine... There was also the challenge of working with unregulated material. Sometimes the distribution of the LSD on the blotter or within the distilled solution provided a stronger-than-anticipated subjective effect, and I would feel compelled to relocate to a more comfortable, enclosed setting. Sometimes my pupils would dilate in such a pronounced way so as to make engagement uncomfortable for myself or others. It was a very fumbly learning curve at first. Fortunately, I underwent this learning with the help of some very understanding people in my life who could assist with monitoring my behavior and growth and stability along the way. And as time went on, I progressed, bit by bit.

If I was going to be interacting with a lot of people, 20 micrograms seemed like a much safer dose. If I was going to be mainly interacting with myself, or one or two people with whom I felt especially comfortable being around, I would take up to 50 micrograms on a given immersion therapy day.

As a point of comparison, longtime LSD therapist and researcher of psychedelic states, Dr. Stan Grof, recently expressed that he found 300-400 micrograms to be the most appropriate dose following his facilitation of literally thousands of LSD-assisted psychotherapy sessions throughout the pre-prohibition era.

In a recent interview with author and established donor to Psychedelic research, Tim Ferris, Grof explained his line of reasoning, stating that "When you use smaller doses, people have more of a chance to resist what happens... if there's areas they don't want to go into, I consider high doses, with proper management, to be more effective therapy." The operative phrase here being "with proper management," as in, supervision and support, in well-monitored environments.

Once again, by contrast, a lot of the work I was doing was, at times, unsupervised, or at least, in less controllable settings, and thus, lower doses seemed to best mitigate the risk. Moreover, on immersion therapy days, I was doing something entirely different from conventional psychotherapeutic approaches. My intention was different. I wasn't trying to plumb the depths of my subconscious to relive the trauma of my own birth. I wasn't trying to sort out my Freudian landscape. I was simply trying to connect more readily with myself and those around me. In this way, I wasn't seeking a visionary experience as much as I was simply seeking an oh-so-subtly enhanced experience of sensorial exactitude.

Along these lines, it's important to note that my approach seems to be a departure on the more conventional approach to psychedelic-assisted therapies as well. In my case, I was exploring my sensory and sociocognitive issues by going out into the world and engaging with others. Most psychedelic-assisted therapies past and present exclusively involve the use of eye masks and headphones in a more private and enclosed environment. Most of these therapies also rely heavily upon inner journeying, which can be a very powerful and transformative experience indeed. And it seems to be that when the eyes are closed, there is a decreased chance of experiencing disorientation, likewise. I say this because the experience of perceiving a shifting, undulating physical environment seen with open eyes is much more jarring than experiencing a dream-like vision with closed eyes. With the eyes closed, any strangeness experienced under the influence of a given psychoactive substance seems to be easier to write off as a dream of some sort, similar to the way a scared child might take comfort in telling itself that the movie is just a movie.

Speaking of challenging experiences...

There were times in which I would be taking a seemingly small therapeutic dose that still altered my perception to the point that an otherwise familiar place would suddenly seem very, very different. But that was also sort of the point of my approach. I was cross-comparing my baseline sociocognitive ASD processing versus my LSD-affected sociocognitive processing. And in order to do that, I needed to interface with the world of people. At times, it was challenging. But I always did what I could to lower risks at every turn.

I put in time, lots of time, researching a wide variety of approaches, case studies, and first-hand accounts, as well as the archived phenomenological reports from the thousands and thousands of psychedelic therapy sessions held in the pre-prohibition era. And this research helped me, a lot. I also spent time reading up on the neuropharmacology of LSD, better knowing my brain and its various features and functionalities from an intellectual vantage point.

Once I began to understand how my various processing centers were being impacted by LSD, I'll admit I lost a little bit of the wonderment associated with my earlier experiences. My reactions shifted from "Woah! Holy Sh%t!" to "Oh, that's my visual processing center synesthetically interacting with another processing center. Ok." And in this way, little by little, what once seemed like magical happenings began to seem more and more like scientifically explainable — and therefore more readily comprehensible — experiential phenomenon.

So yes. I underwent immersion therapy with my eyes and ears and heart center held wide open to the world out there. And as an autistic individual, I saw this type of immersion therapy as the metaphorical equivalent of walking through a dark room with a flashlight in hand. By holding the flashlight of LSD, I became able to learn more immediate, intuitive, internable lessons, like "Oh, that social faux pas I bumped into last time, when the lights were dimmed, was this, or that. Ok, cool. Now I get it. Now I can watch out for that hazard, or that type of action, etc." And so not only could I see more with my LSD flashlight during the time-dependent exposure window, I could also encode the experience as a sense memory and then reference it again, in the future, when my autistic perceptions once again dimmed the lights down on this or that particular subset of stimuli.

On many of my immersion therapy days, I would encounter people in my life and perceive so much more than I saw before. I would experience their expressions with new depth. I would notice if they wanted to be left alone, or if they seemed down. And a certain gentleness became a more normal aspect of my approach. Likewise, I would experience a deeper access to my own depth of feeling when interacting with them. I became more patient, more calm, and more capable of contemplating the weight of the situation. And it was a wonderful time, truly, to re-experience the formerly traumatic landscape of social life, and likewise, little by little, become less and less afraid of situations that used to feel either totally overwhelming, or, paradoxically, totally devoid of actionable clues.

The benefits of the immersion therapy approach were manyfold. For one, I would receive the conventional benefits often mentioned with microdosing LSD, even on therapeutic doses: increased energy, heightened problem solving skills, and a generally rose-tinted (serotonergic) view of what was unfolding. That was all well and good, especially for someone who had lived for so many years in a deeply depressed state. But the real benefit came in the form of being able to participate in meaningful connections with other people, and meaningful inner work within myself.

For reasons yet to be fully explained, LSD seemed to also grant me deep, deep access to not only my emotional senses, but also, to a slightly more far-reaching associative memory bank. So if I was able to decode one particular situation, I seemed to then be able to take that small bit of logic and overlay it on to other moments in the past that weren't exactly the same, but still, similar enough to be able to seem suddenly more comprehensible. In this way, one intuitive realization resulted in clarity for numerous, similar occurrences of fundamental errors in approach.

This type of learning was especially significant in that it was an intuitive process. Because it's one thing to intellectually realize a pattern of behavior, or to be informed by someone else of a particular pattern. But it's a whole 'nother kind of useful to FEEL the impact of the behavior on both yourself and the other individuals in the moment. And it's this type of expanded access to theory-of-mind-enabled empathy that seemed to provide me with lesson after lesson after lesson, most especially in the early days of my self-experimentation.

Another benefit worth noting was the way in which LSD seemed to de-couple my awareness from my subverbal, narrated stream of consciousness. With the aid of LSD, I transitioned from being burdened by my brain to befriending the thoughts that my brain seemed to transceive. When I'd experience a common stressor under the influence of LSD, I seemed to experience a certain spaciousness of thought, similar to what I've experienced in deep meditation in more recent years. Suddenly, I am able to observe myself reacting to the stressor. And in that small opportune window of observance arises the chance to perform multiple mini, surgical-like behavioral interventions, all in real time. It's almost as though LSD allows me to open up my neuro-computer settings and change a few preferences before resuming my regularly scheduled interfacing with the world of human beings.

This process of use-testing and editing my conditioned behavioral responses allowed me to (1) recognize patterns of behavior, (2) consider potential root causes of the behavior (3) consider potential modifications to said behavior, and (4) test and integrate the behavior change IN THE MOMENT. And it's the in-the-moment nature of this approach that made the work feel so powerful. Because normally this type of work would take place in a therapist's office. I would go and say "Hey this happened and it led to this undesired outcome," and the therapist would say "Ok, well, what could you do differently?" and I would say "I could do this or that or this or that?" and they would say "Ok, well, what will you do next time?" and I would say "Umm...I will do this?" and that was great, but the trouble was, I was solving problems that already happened, in the past. And likewise, in talk therapy, I was solving those problems more so from the vantage point of intellect rather than intuition. And this was problematic, or at least, less efficient. Because if the exact situation didn't come up again, discovering the answer didn't seem to be all that useful because my narrow, rigid view of the specific situation prevented me from seeing the broader applications of the insight.

When I arrived at new and novel problems in my pre-LSD life, I seemed to lack the ability to generate new and novel solutions. But then, LSD provided a certain loosening of the mind that helped me improvise in the jam session of life for the simple reason that LSD helped me to hear the other instrumentalists more clearly. In some sense, LSD transformed me from tone-deaf to tone-aware. Simultaneously, LSD gave me the increased processing capacity to not only consider multiple options for reaction and response, but to also visually play out the outcomes in the privacy of my visualizing mind, all while also feeling, emotionally, my reaction to the envisioned outcomes. It's hard to describe unless you've lived it, but, LSD helped me think through live, happening-now situations in the same way a computer can instantaneously generate and test multiple possible answers at once. On LSD, I seem to become a quantum computer of sorts. And it's not literally how it looks through my eyes, but I would describe this type of quantum behavioral problem solving using the following visual metaphor:

Imagine standing in front of two doors. The door on the left: feels familiar; you've walked through it before; "don't talk to that person, just go back home and hide in your room". The door on the right: you haven't walked through before; "talk to the person if you want, they seem bored", and it weirdly also feels familiar, or at least, inviting, for the first time. Then a third door appears that you haven't walked through before; "they're bored but also you don't have to talk to everyone, it's okay to move along", and that too feels like a comfortable option. And then even more doors, countless doors, appear; "why stress about this conversation, you can literally go and do anything you want and change the trajectory of your life plan however you'd like. Woah. Weird." And that door seems oddly approachable, along with a number of other doors. On and on, you notice more doors. And the doors seem to go on and on until suddenly it hits you that there are SO MANY possible doors one can walk through in any given moment; so many more potential paths to walk upon as compared to more automatic, conditioned patterns of behavior. And it's right about then that I'd look back at the first door and think "Weird, this is the only door I walk through, over and over and over all of my life...what's up with that?"...and then I'd realize "Ohhhh this is the safest door..." or "Ohhhhh this door doesn't remind me of the confusion I don't want to experience or the traumatic memory I don't want to recall. That's why I only ever walk through this door. Weird." And this is the power of LSD-assisted therapy, self-guided or otherwise.

With fear levels dialed down and free-form thinking patterns dialed up, I seemed to obtain the critical ability to not only perceive my patterns of conditioning but to also visualize alternatives from a visualizable, dream-like, 3rd-person mind's-eye perspective, experienced in a 1st-person sort of way. In this way, the lens of LSD seemed to grant me an increased ability to notice and alter my patterns of conditioning in ways I could have never otherwise imagined.

If life is a hedge maze, LSD is a helicopter camera that shows me the view from above the hedge maze so that I can see where I am, where I've been, where I'm going, and what rewards or penalties pushed or pulled me toward this particular point in the maze.

And that's how it has seemed to go with LSD-assisted immersion therapy. Over and over and over, this method served as a chance to discover and edit my own conditioning maps. And it's important to point out that these conditioning maps are neither good nor bad. They just...are. Like the carved out paths of a river. They are the well-worn paths of least resistance, generally speaking. They're adaptive. For instance, there's a conditioning map in all of us that tells us "Don't get close to fire, it will burn you!" But if that conditioning is so rigid, we might find ourselves unable to pick up a perfectly useful torch at the entrance to a dark and dangerous tunnel.

In this aforementioned example, our conditioning map tells us, "Don't get close to fire, it will burn you!", but this is an example of potentially "unfit" conditioning in certain circumstances. A conditioning map that says "All fire is to be avoided" isn't serving someone to the fullest. And if they avoid fire entirely, they won't be able to experience the benefits of boiled water, sanitized flatware, properly cooked meat, and on and on. So in this way, I've come to believe that sometimes our ingrained patterns of conditioning and perception keep us safe from possible hazards, physical, psychological, or otherwise. But these same patterns of behavior and belief might also be blocking us from long-ignored pathways that can potentially lead toward joy, elation, growth, and other unforeseen benefits. And so it seemed to be that through LSD-Assisted Immersion

Therapy, I became increasingly aware of my own conditioning, and increasingly capable of arriving at new and novel solutions to new and novel situations.

Over time, I realized that I had formed all sorts of short-cuts to avoid various difficulties. It was as though once upon a childhood I had hit the red button and received a shock, and I experienced confusion, so I stopped looking for red buttons; and I avoided red buttons. In this metaphor, human interactions were the red button that shocked me. They were confusing landmine fields that I believed to be painful, or at the very least, difficult to navigate. So I chose to not navigate them. I avoided the humans. They were the fire I shouldn't get close to. So I didn't. But then LSD lifted this conditioning cage. LSD allowed me to walk through the electric fence. And not only did I survive my walk through the fence. I survived the walk and found joy. I found emotional connection. And yes, sometimes emotional pain was waiting for me on the other side of the fence. But the emotional pain could teach me just as much as the joy. So I walked forward. And with every step forward into formerly unknown domains, I gained an ability to connect more deeply and readily with myself and others.

As I continued to explore the world through the lens of LSD, I realized that I had been living in a perfectly insulated inner world... something of a conceptual prison of sorts. And I didn't know it during my pre-LSD years but this was a wildly limiting approach. I perceived so few options in any given moment. And I limited myself in countless ways. Did I protect myself from the confusion of social encounters? Sure. But did I give myself the chance to improve in any way? No. Absolutely not. And this is where all of this comes together in the form of some very interesting questions...

Did LSD unlock my emotionality or did it open me back up to the emotional experiences that my mind had conditioned me out of pursuing? Was I born unable to experience this arresting level of empathy or was it an adaptive deafening developed very early along in life? I don't know. But these questions themselves wouldn't even be askable if not for the insights made possible via my LSD experiences, most especially because I was often so entrenched in a pattern that I wouldn't be able to recognize it as a pattern at all.

Many of my autistic traits were consistent throughout my life, as confirmed by the witness of my parents. My sensory struggles were consistent. My social ineptitudes were consistent. And my general reclusion and obliviousness to the states of others seemed to be likewise consistent. But even so, I have to wonder. If I wouldn't have resigned myself to hiding in my room for years and years and years, would I have eventually been able to navigate social situations better, earlier in life? Again, I truly don't know the answers to these questions. But what I do know is that regardless of the answers to all of the above, I know for sure that LSD without a doubt gave me the vision and strength that I needed to revisit the formerly stressful process of learning how to human. In this way, LSD gave me the perceptivity I needed to overcome my fears, while at the same time lifting the veil of conceptual thinking so as to grant me direct access to the sensory experience of social existence.

And so the years went by, and I got better and better at not only navigating my life, but also, better and better at dosing with LSD. As is the case with any psychiatric medicine, my approach with LSD required an initial period of titration — as in, the act of gradually increasing or decreasing the dose, dialing it in over time to compensate for any undesired side effects. And even though I've lead with the many benefits of LSD-Assisted Immersion Therapy, that's not to say that I didn't experience some rather unexpected and undesired effects as well.

There are simple and easy to explain effects worth mentioning right off the bat. Firstly, LSD is activating, and thus provides an increase in energy, which is great if you take it in the morning, and not so great for sleep rhythms if taken later in the day. In my experience, LSD had an activation window of anywhere from 10 to 14 hours. So during my days of participating in immersion therapy, I would take a dose of 20-50 micrograms every few days. And I would do so first thing in the morning, when I woke up, so that by the time I readied myself and stepped out to face the world, I was more or less already at the plateau of an experience that would last throughout the day. It was a bit like having a coffee first thing in the morning. But in this case, the effect of the LSD would last me all day, more or less until I returned home and went to sleep.

Now, it's very much worth emphasizing that this approach of taking 20-50 micrograms is NOT the same as microdosing. This dose was taken with the intention of learning about myself and others. This dose engendered very noticeable subjective effects. In this way, I was not using this dose to treat depression, or as a replacement to an SSRI, though it did seem to yield a similar effect.

The biggest difference between microdosing and immersion therapy dosing seems to be that therapeutic doses had a greater tendency to make me tired on the following day. Likewise, the larger doses involved in immersion therapy days engendered more pronounced subjective effects that likewise increased the odds of encountering challenging experiences.

For reasons that I'll explain at another time, there were indeed days when the tab I'd used in the distilled solution was more potent than the one before, and my mind would become more synesthetic (cross-connected) than expected, and I would suddenly find myself greatly irritated by the whirring of an air conditioner, because my auditory processing and kinesthetic processing centers became more intertwined than desired. To combat this potentially distracting effect, I began making rescue tools for myself. I made playlists of exceedingly calm music, and carried a pair of sunglasses just in case my pupils relaxed a bit more than anticipated and made me more sensitive to light. There was a bit of fumbling around in the beginning of this process, absolutely. But ultimately, I found a dose that worked for me in terms of therapeutic application.

I continued to use therapeutic doses in this way, every few days, for some time. And I always did so with intentionality in terms of where I was going and the types of activities in which I would be engaging. For example, I wouldn't take therapeutic doses and go to work. And I wouldn't take a dose on a day in which I was going to have to sit at the DMV, or some other similarly low-vibration environment. And this intentional approach seemed to work well for me. I continued to grow in small and large ways through each and every immersion therapy day. And little by little, life seemed to feel a whole lot more manageable.

Years went by, and despite the immense gains I had made, there came a certain point in time in which the approach felt less and less useful. And it felt this way not because the effect was any less potent, but rather, because I had learned. I had become more sighted, and sensitive, over time.

Armed with an abundance of new insights and a growing backlog of encoded sense memories, I began to shift my attitudes toward a place of held confidence in social settings. In light of this change, I likewise began to wonder if I could go about navigating the world without an LSD regimen of any sort. And this exact pondering brings to light questions that still feel very, very difficult to answer.

Is LSD the boat that takes me across the sea of social confusion, only to then be discarded because the LSD is no longer necessary? Or is LSD more like a unique and irreplaceable boat that keeps me afloat in the forever overwhelming seas of perception as an autistic individual? Ultimately, these questions remain a point of ambiguity for me. And I could go on and on about all the ways I've pondered these questions, but for now, I'll try and state it as directly as possible in saying the following:

On the other side of this LSD-Assisted Immersion Therapy, I felt more connected to myself and others more generally. I still believe that I feel feelings more strongly and perceive more detail on LSD versus NOT on LSD. And I think that might always seem to be the case, for me, given my initial genetic predisposition, my assumed baseline functional connectivity, and the dominance of monotropic processing in my lived experience as an autistic individual. And this is why I refer to LSD as a pair of "Neurological Contact Lenses".

I can remove the lens of LSD and set down the flashlight of LSD and remember the layout of my blurry, dimmed-down living room, and that works, to a point. But there's no substitute for wearing the eyeglasses, or carrying the flashlight, ultimately. And the only reasons I started to wear the lens of LSD less and carry the flashlight of LSD less over time — apart from feeling more confident without LSD — were that (1) LSD was and still is very, very illegal, and (2) LSD could be physiologically harmful in ways we don't yet know of or understand. A given dose may be incredibly small, but repeat use could result in bodily harm we haven't yet discovered.

Speaking of possible risks...

Based on established, peer-reviewed research, LSD appears to have a relatively low neurotoxicity profile and low-risk in terms of physiological effects---mild increases in blood pressure, heart rate, and body temperature are possible, but these effects seem to only become concerning to those with severe, prestanding cardiological issues. Yes of course, psychological trauma is possible if utilizing the drug in an improper setting, or with improper intentions. And there's the very real risk of LSD exacerbating and causing an early onset of other forms of mental illness such as schizophrenia if such an illness is present within a family tree. And even though there is no established lethal dose of LSD, dangerous drug interactions have been documented, and likewise must be considered a very real risk.

In summary: as of the publishing of this text, it is ultimately my firm belief that the practice of self-guided LSD therapy is inherently riskier and therefore inadvisable versus a future model in which regulation and proper screening and monitored, guided administration is possible. As of now, the illicit status of the LSD means there's no way to access proper health screenings; nor is there a way to access LSD that has been synthesized in regulated lab; nor is there a way to have the LSD administered in an environment that minimizes risk to the highest degree, as would be the case in a setting in which facilitators have access and capacity to administer rescue meds and leverage other tools in the event of any unexpected psychological or physiological emergency.

With the aforementioned risks in mind, I reached a point with my work in which I deemed it best to leave the neurological contact lens of LSD behind, for the time being. My LSD experiences with larger doses were life-saving. My LSD experiences with therapeutic doses were life-educating. And my LSD experiences with microdoses were life-stabilizing. But even so, as of the publishing date of this book, LSD is still very, very illegal most everywhere on earth. And I can't enjoy the benefits of my growth if I'm in prison. And so, knowing that I would be publishing this text, I deemed it best to leave LSD behind, for now, and allow the doctors and researchers and therapists to do the work they're trained and qualified to do with medicines they're trained and qualified to research and administer. So in case you missed the giant block of text at the beginning of this book, remember: LSD is still an illegal, Schedule 1 substance in the United States, and that means that LSD cannot be obtained for any purpose, including medicinal and therapeutic use.

Given what I have lived and experienced, I likewise find this scheduling to be absolutely absurd.

CHAPTER SEVEN

WHAT NOW?

Without a doubt, my shift from ASD-impaired processing to LSD-enabled processing represents one of the most — and arguably, THE most — significant awakenings of my life, on par with a blind man's first sighted experience, or to really drive home the metaphor, a deaf man becoming suddenly aware of not only common sounds but also subtler ones, such as that of a dog whistle. And for however amazing this transformation may be, the science is still out on exactly how any of this is possible.

Once again: I am not a neuropsychopharmocologist. I am just a hyper-interested autistic individual who experienced profound increases in perception relative to critical fail points in my social processing. As such, I am inclined to say that my anecdotal experience is very much worth voicing. Because we know from FMRI and MEG studies that drugs such as LSD and psilocybin possess the ability to boost cross-talk between key processing centers. Studies utilizing similar imaging technology have also helped us to arrive at the theory that ASD is most likely resultant from — or at least, related to — weak or deafened cross-talk between key processing centers.

With all of this in mind, I find it critical to bring my story out into the world. Because the science seems to make sense on paper. And in real life — in this life I live — the neuropsychopharmacological effects of LSD literally makes sense. As in, LSD makes me SENSE that which was previously inaccessible to me and my awareness.

Me Not on LSD:
"That woman's smile indicates she is happy"
Me on LSD:
"I feel happiness in the presence of this smiling woman"

* Although the difference between these two statements may seem subtle, please bear in mind that I am attempting to describe the difference between knowing I'm alive and feeling alive, period.

Thanks to LSD, I have become suddenly and viscerally aware of body language, intention, facial expressions, and countless other bits of sensory data that I was previously blind to perceiving throughout my entire life. And I don't know if I can stress the significance of this if I wrote ten thousand more books on the topic. But in the interest of all those autistic individuals who've struggled to understand human behavior or who feel overwhelmed or confused by the simplest of social exchanges, I must, at the very least, recommend that researchers explore the neuropsychopharmacological intersection of ASD and LSD.

My first-hand experiences with LSD have been far too meaningful and educational and repeatable for me to not share what I have lived. The ideas I'm expressing are not based on one experience, or even a few experiences such as this. No.

These beliefs are founded upon first-hand evidence gleaned amidst hundreds of days of experiencing the world through the lens of LSD.

By introducing a few millionths of a gram of LSD into my system, I become able to live the human experience in ways I could have never imagined. And I mean that in the most literal of ways. Someone could've tried to explain the experience of polytropic empathetic processing to me all day everyday and I still wouldn't have been able to fully grasp the gravity of this shift, for the same reason a colorblind man can't imagine what it's like to see color. But anyone who's ever seen those videos of colorblind people putting on specialized glasses that enable them to see the world in full color already knows how joyous such a moment can be for the newly full-color-sighted individual. Truly, if not for LSD, I would have never been able to fully experience the beauty and utility of feeling my way forward.

And so I must say, with the purest of heart, that LSD has been a blessing in my life. So pardon my yelling and also my redundancy but........

LSD

LET ME

SEE

&

COMPREHEND

COMPLICATED!

SOCIAL

BEHAVIORS.

LSD LET ME

FEEL

FEELINGS

&

DEEPLY

SENSE

THE

FEELINGS

OF

OTHER.

LIVING.

BEINGS.

FROM A SINGLE DOSE,

I WOKE UP

FROM A
NUMB & DEAFENED,
BLACK & WHITE LIFE,
OBSCURED BY MEMORIZED MAPS,

&

I FELL IN LOVE

WITH
THE
D-Y-N-A-M-I-C
FULL-COLOR,
HEART-TINGLING,
SENSATIONAL,
VIBRATIONAL,
EXPRESSIVE

WORLD

OF
HUMAN BEINGS BEING SOCIAL

SO PLEASE

-PRETTY PLEASE-

WITH AN fMRI IMAGE ON TOP

P L E A S E

C O N S I D E R

RESCHEDULING LSD

S O   W E   C A N

MORE READILY

R E S E A R C H

L S D

` , ` , (

Because I believe. Yes. I believe with all of my being that these shifts in awareness are worthy of our attention, our research, and indeed, our funding & support.

CHAPTER EIGHT

LSD RESEARCH, THEN & NOW

At this point, I think I speak for both you, the reader, and me, the writer, in saying that we both get the main point of this text: "LSD seems to have enabled me to experience polytropic processing, deeply felt empathy, social cue recognition, and general relief from my particular ASD-related sensory issues. Also, LSD-Assisted Immersion Therapy helped me to navigate my concurrent depressive symptoms, while at the same time helping me to alter conditioned patterns of behavior in pursuit of a more self-aware, peer-connected social existence". Cool. Great. Awesome. That's great. The previous ideas might be new to you, but they aren't very new to me. I've lived this. And now comes the part that is very new to both you and me: the part where we attempt to arrive at a scientific understanding of how these shifts in perception are even possible from a neuropsychopharmacological perspective.

As far as established research goes, there is a large pool of data available to us relative to ASD, and a small but growing pool of data available to us relative to LSD and other tryptamine psychedelics such as psilocybin. There is A LOT more research relative to ASD versus psychedelics in general, largely as a result of drug prohibition in the US and abroad.

In this way, if the research I present in this chapter seems a bit far-reaching, it's just as much a result of a lack of scientific access to these compounds as it is the frontier nature of my personal exploration of autism... on acid.

In my personal deep-dive into the archives, I was only able to track down one small batch of studies, conducted in the early 1960's, that directly explores the administration of LSD in autistic individuals, and we'll touch on those studies in a moment. Likewise, as far as I could search, there is yet to be any neuroimaging study involving the administration of LSD with autistic individuals. Ultimately, a study such as this seems to be the most likely to bring about answers to the questions I am proposing in this text. But we're not there yet. Maybe someday we will be... but for now, the best I can do is present findings that hint at some of the potential correlations between the measurable neuropharmacologic properties of LSD and the theorized neural signatures and biomarkers of ASD.

Regarding the sourcing of research... Everything in this chapter was searched and discovered via pubmed.gov, a publicly accessible archive of peer-reviewed biomedical publications. Links to full publications appear below the heading of each respective article mentioned in this chapter.

Last but not least: all of this is presented with the aim of perpetuating discussion. At the end of this book, you'll find a link to a Google Document version of this text, shared in full, for free, on the internet, with permissions allowing for comments. I encourage anyone from any side of this discussion to visit this document and leave a comment. You can even tag @autismonacid@gmail.com and I'll join you in the discussion.

Above all, it is my hope that a multidisciplinary, world-wide collaboration such as this — comprised of researchers, pharmacologists, neuroscientists, therapists, caretakers, and autistic individuals connecting the dots, together, and participating in a meaningful dialogue — will result in a more well-rounded and complete understanding of the neuropsychopharmacological underpinnings of everything I've described in this text.

And so without any further adieu, let's jump into the curated research studies, beginning first with a deep dive into the archives of the pre-prohibition era of psychedelic studies...

The Use of Psychedelic Agents With Autistic Schizophrenic Children

Originally Published in *Psychedelic Review*, 1969

Link to Article:

https://bibliography.maps.org/bibliography/default/resource/4639

Why This Research Stood Out To Me:

As far as my personal search has gone, this appears to be the only published mention of pharmacotherapeutic treatment of sociocognitive deficits through the administration of LSD in a medical research setting. These particular studies contained a number of issues, as discussed in the summary and conclusions section posted below. And so I present this information with a very skeptical delivery. The studies are far from rigorous in terms of the controls and standards of modern research. But given the novel nature of this study, and the direct overlap with the subject at hand, it seems worthy of inclusion in this exploratory chapter.

Abstract (Directly Quoted):

"Seven independent studies are reviewed involving a total of 91 austistic schizophrenic children who had been given psychedelic drugs for therapeutic and/or experimental purposes. A variety of psychedelic agents, dosage levels, frequency of administrations, and treatment schedules were employed. The most effective results were obtained with at least

100 μg doses of LSD-25 given daily or weekly over relatively extended periods of time. Although each of these studies contained therapeutic and experimental flaws, it was concluded that the collective findings argue strongly for more extensive applications of psychedelic drugs in the treatment of austistic children."

Select Quotes from Researchers:

"...the vocabularies of several of the children increased after LSD or UML; several seemed to be attempting to form words or watched adults carefully as they spoke; many seemed to comprehend speech for the first time or were able to communicate their needs... Very few of these changes in communication had been noted previously in such a large number of children, and at such a relatively rapid rate..."

"They appeared flushed, bright eyed, and unusually interested in the environment... They participated with increasing eagerness in motility play with adults and other children... They seek positive contacts with adults, approaching them with face uplifted and bright eyes, and responding to fondling, affection, etc..."

"Some showed changes in facial expression in appropriate reactions to situations for the first time."

Summary and Conclusions:

(Direct Quote from Publication)

1. Seven independent studies are reviewed involving a total of 91 austistic schizophrenic children who had been given psychedelic drugs for therapeutic and/or experimental purposes.

2. The large majority of children treated in these studies were between six and ten years of age and were completely refractory to all other forms of treatment.

3. There was only slight indication of any differential response or benefit as a function of age, diagnosis, duration or severity of illness.

4. A variety of psychedelic agents, dosage levels, frequency of administrations, and treatment schedules were employed. The most effective results were obtained with at least 100 microgram doses of LSD-25 given daily or weekly over relatively extended periods of time.

5. Concerning the physical and psychological milieu, greater therapeutic benefit was related to: (a) the degree of active therapist involvement with the patient; (b) an opportunity to experience meaningful objects and interpersonal activities; and (c) congenial settings that were reasonably free of artificiality, experimental or medical restrictions, and mechanically administered procedures.

6. The most consistent effects of psychedelic therapy reported in these studies included: (a) improved speech behavior in otherwise mute children; (b) increased emotional responsiveness to other children and adults; (c) an elevation in positive mood including frequent laughter; and (d) decreases in compulsive ritualistic behavior.

7. Differences in patient attributes, treatment technique, research design, and other non- drug factors seemed to affect the frequency and stability of favorable outcomes. The types of improvement found were essentially the same in each study.

8. Although each of these studies contained serious therapeutic and experimental flaws, it was concluded that the collective findings argue strongly for more extensive applications of psychedelic drugs in the treatment of austistic children.

Identification of Neural Connectivity Signatures of Autism Using Machine Learning

Originally Published in *Frontiers in Neuroscience*, 2013

Link to Article:

https://www.frontiersin.org/articles/10.3389/fnhum.2013.00670/full

Abstract (Directly Quoted):

"Alterations in interregional neural connectivity have been suggested as a signature of the pathobiology of autism. There have been many reports of functional and anatomical connectivity being altered while individuals with autism are engaged in complex cognitive and social tasks. Although disrupted instantaneous correlation between cortical regions observed from functional MRI is considered to be an explanatory model for autism, the causal influence of a brain area on another (effective connectivity) is a vital link missing in these studies. The current study focuses on addressing this in an fMRI study of Theory-of-Mind (ToM) in 15 high-functioning adolescents and adults with autism and 15 typically developing control participants. Participants viewed a series of comic strip vignettes in the MRI scanner and were asked to choose the most logical end to the story from three alternatives, separately for trials involving physical and intentional causality."

Why This Research Stood Out to Me:

This study showed a correlation between low or weak between-brain-region connectivity and autistic diagnosis. This relationship is especially significant when we start to examine the pharmacological effects of LSD in terms of increasing between-brain-region connectivity across numerous regions. This study also produced a readily accessible visualization of the effective connectivity of autistic individuals versus "typically developing" individuals...

In the words of Dr. Kana, the project's senior researcher...

> "This research suggests brain connectivity as a neural signature of autism and may eventually support clinical testing for autism... We found the information transfer between brain areas, causal influence of one brain area on another, to be weaker in autism... We can see that there are consistently weaker brain regions due to the disrupted brain connectivity... There's a very clear difference." https://www.uab.edu/news/research/item/3861-research-finds-brain-scans-may-aid-in-diagnosis-of-autism

The following figure illustrates the results of this study. As stated in the published article...

> "The width of the arrows represents the path strength and the color of the path indicates its rank obtained during classification with 1 being the most significant and 19 being the least significant."

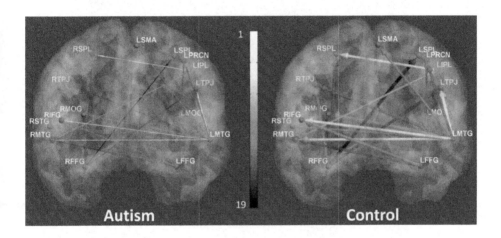

And just in case the above image is hard for you to see, I've scaled up the figure on the following page. Again, the most important takeaway here is how the overall strength of connections appears to be significantly stronger in the neural pathways of the control versus the autistic group.

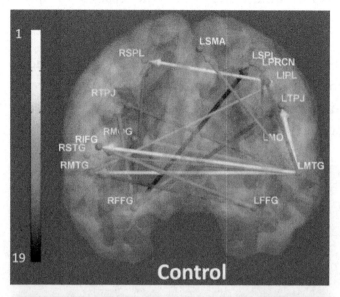

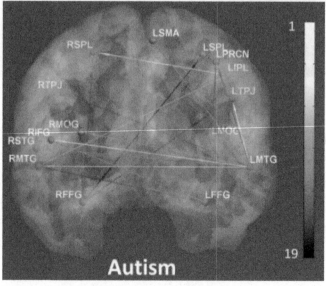

Neural Correlates of The LSD Experience Revealed by Multimodal Neuroimaging

Originally Published in
Proceedings of The National Academy of Sciences, April, 2016

Link to Article: https://www.pnas.org/content/113/17/4853

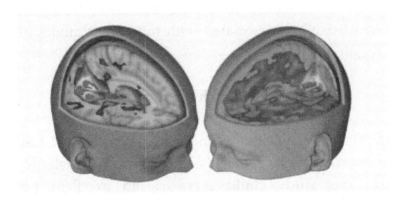

Summary:

After a decades-long prohibition-impacted gap in LSD research, the world received a glimpse of the first ever published neuroimaging scans of the brain under the influence of LSD. This landmark study, made possible through a partnership between The Beckley Foundation and the Imperial Research Programme of Imperial College UK, provided numerous insights into the neuropharmacological effects of LSD. And one of the most interesting findings discusses the surprising effect that LSD seemed to play on the Default Mode Network...

According to the study ...and this is a direct quote from The Beckley Foundation's website....

"...the DMN disintegrates under LSD, allowing for a magnificent increase in communication between brain networks that are normally highly segregated. This produces a more integrated pattern of connectivity throughout the entire brain, which may be associated with more fluid modes of cognition...."

Why This Research Stood Out To Me:

By exploring the synesthesia-inducing properties of LSD, and the noteworthy impact that LSD has on the Default Mode Network, this study could serve as an excellent point of consideration when cross-comparing the neural correlates of LSD and ASD. From a subjective standpoint, research such as this could also potentially aid in explaining the neuropharmacological roots of my LSD-induced onset of newly amplified cross-communication between my kinesthetic, visual, emotional, and memory-based processing---a tethering that in turn results in intuitive polytropic processing and awareness in the context of interpersonal navigation. This research also stands out because of the previously mentioned study detailing the correlation between low between-brain-region connectivity and autistic diagnosis. Could LSD and other tryptamine psychedelics like psilocybin be the pharmacological turnkey to boosting the strength of cross-talk in autistic individuals in a time-dependent or long-term, sustainable fashion?

LSD Acutely Impairs Fear Recognition & Enhances Emotional Empathy & Sociality

Originally Published in
The Official Journal of The American College of Neuropsychopharmacology, June, 2016

Link to Article: https://www.nature.com/articles/npp201682

Abstract (Directly Quoted):

"Lysergic acid diethylamide (LSD) is used recreationally & has been evaluated as an adjunct to psychotherapy to treat anxiety in patients with life-threatening illness. LSD is well-known to induce perceptual alterations, but unknown is whether LSD alters emotional processing in ways that can support psychotherapy. We investigated the acute effects of LSD on emotional processing using the Face Emotion Recognition Task (FERT) & Multifaceted Empathy Test (MET). The effects of LSD on social behavior were tested using the Social Value Orientation (SVO) test. Two similar placebo-controlled, double-blind, random-order, crossover studies were conducted using 100 μg LSD in 24 subjects and 200 μg LSD in 16 subjects (20. All of the subjects were healthy & mostly hallucinogen-naive 25- to 65-year-old volunteers."

Abstract Continued... (Directly Quoted):

"LSD produced feelings of happiness, trust, closeness to others, enhanced explicit & implicit emotional empathy on the MET, & impaired the recognition of sad & fearful faces on the FERT. LSD enhanced the participants' desire to be with other people & increased their prosocial behavior on the SVO test. These effects of LSD on emotion processing & sociality may be useful for LSD-assisted psychotherapy."

Why This Research Stood Out To Me:

This study more than any other helps to support my first-hand experiences in terms of detecting measurable increases in emotional empathy and sociality. This study also offers some degree of evidence-based support for my experienced successes in the domains of LSD-Assisted Immersion Therapy. The day that I encountered this particular article, I found a peace within myself. The subjective effects that I had lived and experienced had been consistently found in the minds of others. Yes, there is still a ton to explore and refine. But studies such as this go a long way in terms of validating my first-hand account.

– –

CHAPTER NINE

AN OPEN LETTER TO SCIENCE

In the wake of what is now approaching a half-century of LSD prohibition, LSD remains almost entirely off limits in the United States for any given purpose, including not only medicinal and therapeutic use, but also, critically, scientific research. The few formal studies mentioned in the previous chapter were only made possible by groups based outside of the U.S., with studies most often funded almost exclusively through private and crowd-funded donations.

As I mentioned numerous times in this text, very little is known about the longitudinal effect of the routine administration of LSD. Yes, we have a reasonable idea of LSD's relative harmlessness based on the estimated millions of doses of LSD taken since the drug's discovery, coupled with anecdotal evidence — such as how LSD's inventor, Albert Hoffman, an advocate and frequent explorer of LSD, lived to a healthy 102 years old. Even so, we still find ourselves in a bizarre point in history in which we know so very little about a compound that has taught so very many of us so very much.

Fortunately, however, the tides are turning...

Registered Clinical Trials
with classical psychedelics

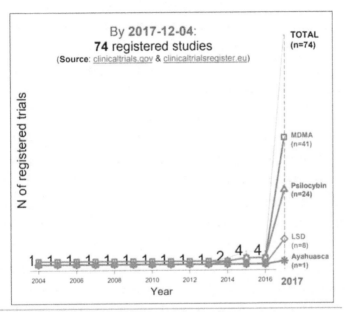

Thanks to the power of the Internet, and a combination of crowd-funded and crowd-sourced research studies, as well as the relatively new infusion of private donor capital into psychedelic research, work of this sort has finally re-entered the mainstream conversation in a very real way. And this resurgence is picking up speed with each passing day.

The shifting stigma and move toward legitimate research made possible by various organizations — Including The Multidisciplinary Association of Psychedelic Studies, The Heffter Institute, The Beckley Foundation, and The Johns Hopkins Center for Psychedelic and Consciousness Research, among many others — simultaneously normalizes this research while at the same time making stories such as mine all the more essential in terms of guiding future studies. And I am filled with gratitude for the effort that has been put forth up to this point by ambitious researchers as well as those who have stepped up to voice their truth despite the legal landscape. All of this collective effort has helped to create a climate in which stories and ideas — like the one I am sharing with you, right now — can be shared without fear by those who feel compelled to do so.

If I had a wish, I would wish that neuroimaging studies could continue to provide insight into what exactly happens during the psychedelic experience. I would wish that such studies could continue to reveal not only the neurological underpinnings of both psychedelic and autistic experiences, but also, in turn, the neurological underpinnings of the broader human experience. Because I strongly believe that by studying psychedelics and autism, we advance our perspective on the formation of perspectives, period. And I for one find that to be an exciting prospect indeed.

In order to accomplish this kind of progress in the domain of psychedelic and autistic research, there will need to be continued support from all fronts. As more and more researchers explore these molecules from a neuropsychopharmacological perspective, patients and practitioners from all sectors will always have the option to offer support, not only through funding but also via open discussions on social media, in cafes and coffee shops, and at most any location on earth in which it is still legal to discuss ideas.

As evidenced by my own participation in the Chicago-based MeetUp group, Psychedelics and The Future of Psychiatry, as well as my most recent invitations from Aware Project Los Angeles and the Psychedelics Today podcast to speak publicly about my story... the negative stigma surrounding LSD and other psychedelics seems to be shifting from fear-based to fact-aware. And it is my hope that we can all mature and discuss these formerly controversial compounds just as we would any other form of medicine.

I acknowledge that I am taking a risk any time I declare my support for further research into LSD-assisted therapy as well as the potential routine use of LSD for the treatment of symptoms and behaviors and processing difficulties common in autistic individuals. I acknowledge that I have taken risks from the very beginning of my self-experimentation and discovery phase. And I wouldn't have taken such risks if I wasn't fueled by such a strong sense of dissatisfaction in my pre-LSD life. In some sense, I felt like a food critic who hadn't yet grown a tongue; bitter and angry and confused by what all the hoopla about being alive was all about. But now. Now. NOW! I am a grateful observer and joyous participant in this dance. I owe my life to LSD, and remain hopeful for our culture's ability to revisit and reinvestigate the potential benefit of studying the intersection of neurodivergence and psychedelic experiences.

With Love and Gratitude,
-Aaron Paul Orsini

CONNECT WITH ME

Hi.

I wrote this text in hopes of sharing my story & helping us all get one step closer to asking & answering some very big questions related to both ASD & LSD.

If this writing speaks to you, your experience, or your expertise, or if you're aware of any research or relevant opportunities that might assist us all in answering or refining some of the questions & theories proposed in this text, please send an Email to autismonacid@gmail.com.

For more information about this book, or to watch & listen to my latest keynote speeches & interviews on this exact topic, please visit www.AutismOnAcid.com.

For more stories like this or for opportunities to connect & learn alongside other neurodivergent individuals, please visit AutisticPsychedelic.com, where you'll also find an abundance of additional resources, chat forums, survey opportunities, & other ways of supporting this ongoing, community-fueled effort.

Thank you so much for your time and consideration.

-Aaron Paul Orsini

NOTE ABOUT EDITIONS

As of February 20th, 2020, the title of this book has been updated from "Autism on Acid: How LSD Helped Me Bridge The ASD-Neurotypical Divide" to instead include a replacement subtitle: "How LSD Helped Me Understand, Navigate, Alter & Appreciate My Autistic Perceptions"

This change in phrasing---however small it may seem---is very important to me as an autistic individual and a member of the autism advocacy community. And I will explain this change in the following way:

In the months after my first sharing of this work, messages began to pour in from individuals who had experienced similar alterations in perception. And that was and always will be great to hear. But there were other messages from caretakers or autistics who seemed to be interested in my work for perhaps unhelpful or at least, more potentially burdensome reasons.

So why the new title? Well... put simply, as this memoir outlines (hopefully!), LSD helped me understand, navigate, alter and appreciate my autistic perceptions. And the most curious pair of words in that string (in my opinion) seems to be "alter"+"appreciate" because even though such a pairing may seem contradictory, it makes a lot of sense to me, because I've come to understand the benefits of not being on LSD as an autistic individual in addition to the benefits of being on LSD as an autistic individual. This doesn't make my support for my practice and exploration any less strong. I'm simply trying to color in the nuance and bring even more balance to the story.

Just as a person with a hearing impairment can insert an assistive, hearing-altering device and appreciate a symphony, so too can that same person with a hearing impairment remove an assistive hearing device and appreciate silence, Similarly, I can add an assistive dose of LSD and appreciate the symphony of socializations and intensely felt emotions, just as I can remove an assistive dose of LSD and appreciate the muting of emotional intensity and the symphony of neverending brainstorming & nonstop analytic problem solving bouncing around inside my skull. And that's why and how the terms "alter" and "accept" manage to coexist in the title of this book.

Before LSD, the nonstop brainstorming seemed to be a burden. Now, this nonstop brainstorming can be cultivated and applied for a variety of uses, such as writing this book. Even so, between my explorations of both LSD and meditation, I've also become aware of the benefits of mental quieting. LSD helps me quiet my mind, yes. But so does limiting my caffeine intake. So again, it comes back to intention.

What is the task at hand? What tool am I picking up to solve it? How does the picking up of this tool versus this tool impact my ability to not only solve the problem but also SELECT or NOTICE a given problem from a perhaps infinite list of potential threats that my awareness might notice?

Without LSD, the most important task at a party used to be figuring out the most efficient transportation options to and from the party. With LSD, the most important task at a party becomes saying hello and swimming in the energies of human interaction. So which one is better? Neither! They're both helpful states of perception!

A lot of the problems my younger self experienced seemed to stem from reaching toward the mythical target of "normalcy". But the more time I spent with everything, including LSD, the more I realized that one of the biggest weights I self-forced myself to lift everyday was the burden of believing I wasn't "normal enough" yet. But that weight and stress was some real heavy, self-created, culturally-reinforced stress, akin to the difficulties experienced by a fish that walks around a forest hoping to prove it can climb trees rather than flourishing under the sea where it's body and mind can feel at ease. Again, in my instance, LSD helped me navigate the forest; LSD helped me, a fish out of water, feel at home on land. But I was still raised under the sea, in the comfort of my introverted autistic inner world. So there's an unavoidable gravity I experience toward this youthful, under-the-sea space, even if I've adapted to learning how to breathe out of water.

To be clear, there seems to still be a more medical-model-specific or neuroscience-research-language-related utility in stating that LSD made my perceptions seem more "neurotypical" or that LSD perhaps helped me process stimuli in a manner similar to "typically developing subjects". And I state this in various ways throughout the book, discussing how LSD gave me a chance to hone polytropic processing and other newly available neurological capabilities. But even so, it still seems potentially unhelpful to proliferate the belief that autistic individuals (or any individuals) need to be or act "more normal". Yes, shared or at least resemblant social behaviors seem to be essential to any cohabitating species, but so too is nature's essential and not-so-secret ingredient: diversity. And so I choose to identify with the neurodiversity movement, and to likewise encourage any autistic individual or caretaker to pause for a moment and accept the way things seem to be, already, so that they can work toward accepting or rejecting the work involved in making a change. In other words, before we go about rushing to change an autistic person, let's at least take a deep dive into accepting their language, their expressions, and yes, their difficulties, and yes, tools that could be assistive in navigating all of the above. It's cliche I know but acceptance is the first step toward meaningful growth for autistics and caretakers and humans of any sort. And I know this because I didn't make any real progress until I accepted so many aspects of my predispositions. So here I am. I accept me. I accept that my views on this topic need not be anyone else's views. I'm just explaining a complex topic in the name of love for anyone out there who views themself or someone they love as "needing to change" rather than "potentially open to choosing to change".

No two autistics (or non-autistics) are exactly alike. And the label of ASD specifically seems to have been stretched further and further over time to the point that it now includes persons with so many varied symptoms that it's perhaps more useful to discuss these things in terms of self-identified or clinician-identified behaviors and or self-identified or clinician-identified culturally-relevant advantages or disadvantages and do away with umbrella categories all the same. These labels are useful, to a point. Just as words are useful, to a point. And I know, diagnoses are crucial to things like medical benefits, etc. So yes, we will continue to debate these topics. I'm sure. But in the interest of staying in my lane here, I bring this all back to center in stating that **the identities and labeling approaches within the autism community are so very, very, VERY complicated.**

In light of this complexity, and the focus of this particular piece of writing devoted to intersection of psychedelics and autism, I will not even attempt to speak on behalf of other autistics, or should I say autistic individuals (?), people with autism (?), people on the spectrum (?), people with autism spectrum disorder (?), non-neurotypical people (?), etc., because even though it may sound like I'm joking around, this is serious. So serious. And yes, there is utility in diagnosis. But I remain an open advocate for individuals who want to use whatever language they prefer to utilize in terms of how they relate to their formal diagnosis.

:: In breath. Out breath. ::

In summary: I speak on behalf of myself. I speak on behalf of my own experience.

And so, again, to bring it back to center:

I changed the title of this book because I wanted to emphasize that LSD changed me but didn't make me "normal" or "more normal". LSD just helped me to better comprehend whatever was going on in the world of human beings living and speaking and socializing around me. Because before LSD, I was confused. But then LSD brought clarity. And yes, LSD altered my perceptions. But these alterations weren't unidirectional. I didn't go from abnormal to normal and say, "Ta-Da, all perfect now! Hooray!" No. I just changed seats in the concert hall. The same orchestra's still playing on stage. But the acoustics seem different over here, in this new seat, now. And that's great. But so too was my seat over there, before I took LSD. I just didn't realize it then, because I was so focused on finding a new/better seat that I didn't even think to appreciate the seat in which I was sitting. Don't get me wrong, sometimes my old seat was also miserable for more basic reasons, like sensitivities gone haywire. But I can't emphasize enough how helpful it has been to simply become aware of my neurological peculiarities through the lens of LSD. It's a bit like the fish that suddenly realizes it's been in water its whole life; simultaneously surprising and yet somehow, paradoxically, not-so-surprising just the same.

So yes. LSD helped me understand "neurotypical behaviors" a bit better. But these behaviors are no better nor worse than "autistic behaviors". It's all just agreements forged between people like you and me and everybody. And so I encourage all of us to be open to the learning of the language of autistics, just as I would encourage we so-called "autistics" to remain open to learning the language of so-called "neurotypicals". I could go on and on about this, but I'll pause here.

If anything I've written here seems off-putting, let's talk about that, together. I'm here to hear you out. I'm here to listen to most any take on these subjects. This is a discussion. There's a whole big internet to host us now. So no worries. We can converse about this for as long as we'd like to converse :)

And yeah, this will take time. It will always take time. Understanding one another always takes time. Especially if we're working with only words. Because when we're working with only words, we all bring our own respective, personal relationship to these words in terms of associated connotations, meanings, etc. So yes. We are ABSOLUTELY going to misunderstand one another. And that's fine. That's... normal ;)

Thank you for reading.

Now.

Let's get on with the collaboration & research, yeah?

autismonacid@gmail.com
twitter.com/autismonacid
instagram.com/autismonacid
www.autisticpsychedelic.com
www.autismonacid.com

READING LIST

It is with tremendous gratitude that I acknowledge the wisdom contained in the following books, all of which assisted me greatly amidst my pursuit of comprehending the peculiar and unique perspectives engendered by both ASD and LSD.

The Complete Guide to Asperger's Syndrome by Tony Attwood
Frontiers of Psychedelic Consciousness by David Brown
Mindblindness: An Essay on Autism and Theory of Mind by Simon Baron-Cohen
The Psychedelic Explorer's Guide by James Fadiman
Animals in Translation by Temple Grandin
Thinking in Pictures: My Life with Autism by Temple Grandin
LSD: Doorway to the Numinous by Stanislav Grof
LSD Psychotherapy by Stan Grof
Listening to Ayahuasca by Rachel Harris
LSD and The Divine Scientist by Albert Hoffman
LSD: My Problem Child by Albert Hoffman
Heads: A Biography of Psychedelic America by Jesse Jarnow
I Think I Might Be Autistic by Cynthia Kim
Changing Our Minds by Don Lattin
Drugs Without The Hot Air by David Nutt
Overtones and Undercurrents by Ralph Metzner
Psychedelic Medicine by Richard Louise Miller
Look Me in The Eye: My Life With Asperger's by John Elder Robinson
Be Different: My Adventures with Asperger's by John Elder Robinson
Acid Test by Tom Schroder
PIHKAL: A Chemical Love Story by Alexander Shulgrin
TIHKAL: The Continuation by Alexander Shulgrin
Neurotribes: The Legacy of Autism & The Future of Neurodiversity
by Steve Silberman
Born on a Blue Day: Inside The Extraordinary Mind of an Autistic Savant
by Daniel Tammet
A Really Good Day: How Microdosing Made a Mega Difference in My Mood,
My Marriage, and My Life
by Ayelet Waldman
How to Change Your Mind: What The New Science of Psychedelics Teaches Us
About Consciousness, Dying, Addiction, Depression, and Transcendence
by Michael Pollan

Made in the USA
Middletown, DE
01 October 2023